Tigris River

Nineveh

Euphrates River

Antioch

Sidon

Tyre

Dan

Damascus

CANAAN

Capernaum

Sea of
Galilee

River Jordan

Nazareth

Endor

Joppa

BABYLON

Mt. of Olives

Samaria

Jericho

Bethany

Gethsemane

Jerusalem

Bamoth
Gilead

Timnath

Bethlehem

Mt. Nebo

Gaza

Gath

JUDEA

PHILISTIA

Hebron

Dead Sea

MOAB

Beersheba

EDOM

Gomorrah

Sodom

The Garden of Eden

They went out from the ark and saw that the land was dry. (Page 8)

The Golden Book of
BIBLE STORIES

FAVORITE STORIES FROM THE OLD
AND NEW TESTAMENTS RETOLD FOR CHILDREN

With a foreword by CHARLES M. SHELDON

Author of IN HIS STEPS

With 31 Illustrations in color
by C. E. *and* H. M. BROCK

GROSSET & DUNLAP

Publishers   New York

Printed in the United States of America

God's Fingerprints

A Foreword to *The Golden Book of Bible Stories*

by CHARLES M. SHELDON
Author of *In His Steps*

HAVE YOU EVER SAT IN A CAR NEAR THE curb in a big city and watched the people as they passed? If you have done this, you have noticed that no two persons are alike. Each person has a different face; no two have exactly the same kind of nose or forehead or chin. All are different.

If you could take the fingerprints of all these strangers you would find, too, that each of them has fingerprints of his own—fingerprints like those of no one else in the world. And then you would realize more than ever how different are all the people who are alive today.

But think of all the fingerprints that God has made since the day of the Creation! And think how each of them has represented a single person—a king, a slave, a mother, a thief, a child, an old man, a shepherd boy, an explorer, a scientist, a business man!

You have heard that the Bible is the most wonderful book in the world. It tells the stories of many, many "fingerprints"—not imaginary people, not strange or dull ones, but people who had hopes and fears, joys and griefs, just like ours. The more we read about them the more we understand that, although they are all interesting and different, they are all human like us. Woodrow Wilson was right when he called the Bible the "word of life," a book peopled by thousands of real men and women and children.

The people of the Bible lived long ago. Jesus himself never saw a church, a public school, an airplane, a subway, a telephone, a printing press, or many other things that we all are familiar with today. Few if any of the Bible's people could have imagined such things as the motion picture or radio or electric light. Yet when we read about them we feel close to them; it does not seem to matter that they lived thousands of years ago. Like us, they knew what it is to be alive.

And that is why Bible stories such as the ones to be found in this book will never grow old. They are the stories of people who were God's children as we are, who chose between right and wrong day by day, who had in their hearts the thoughts and feelings that make life happy or unhappy, worthwhile or useless. These people are all different, but they are all God's fingerprints.

Many people of the Bible were heroes and heroines, and the stories of their lives should inspire us today. As you read these stories you will see how men and women and children of long ago struggled for what they believed was good, and were rewarded. This is possible for us today as it was for them. For we, too, are fingerprints of God.

Contents

THE OLD TESTAMENT

CONTENTS

CONTENTS

CONTENTS

Color Plates

COLOR PLATES

The Old Testament

Abraham joyously loosed his son's bonds. (Page 14)

He saw before him a golden ladder. (Page 22)

In the Beginning

IN THE BEGINNING GOD CREATED HEAVEN and earth. The earth had no form and everything was dark. So God said, "Let there be light." And there was light. When God saw the light, He found that it was good, so He divided the light from the darkness. He called the light Day, and He called the darkness Night. The evening and the morning were the first day.

On the second day, God put the skies above the water, and He called this space Heaven. Another evening and morning passed, bringing the third day.

Then God gathered the waters together to let the dry land appear. The dry land God called Earth, and the gathering together of the waters He called Seas. As He looked at the earth, God said, "Let the earth bring forth grass that will yield seed, and trees that will bear fruit, with seeds that will grow into more trees after their own kind." And the earth brought forth grass and flowers and fruit trees, and God said that it was good.

On the fourth day God said, "Let there be lights in the skies to divide day from night. Let them be for signs and for seasons and for days and years, and let them give light upon the earth."

God made two great lights, the greater light to rule the day, and the lesser light to rule the night, and He made the stars, also. God set them in the skies to give light upon the earth and to divide the light from the darkness.

Another night passed, and on the fifth morning God said, "Let the waters bring forth many creatures that move, and fowl that may fly about in the open skies."

Then God created great whales, and all kinds of fish and creatures that moved in the seas, and every winged bird in the sky. He looked at them and blessed them, saying, "Be fruitful and multiply, and fill the waters in the seas, and let the fowl multiply on the earth."

On the sixth day God made all the beasts of the earth and creatures that creep on the ground. Then God said, "Let us make man, in My image. And let him rule over the fish of the sea, and over the fowl of the air, and over the beasts and every creeping thing, and over all the earth."

So God created man and blessed him and said, "Behold! I have given you every herb on the face of the earth, and trees with seed-bearing fruit for you to eat."

And God saw everything that He had made, and found it very good. So ended the sixth day.

On the seventh day God rested. He blessed the seventh day and made it holy because it was His day of rest.

Adam and Eve

GOD HAD NOT CAUSED ANY RAIN TO FALL on the earth, but a mist came up and watered the ground so that everything grew. Then in Eden, God planted a garden, and there He put the man He had made. He planted every beautiful tree and bush, and all those that were good for food. In the midst of the garden He planted the tree of life and the tree of knowledge of good and evil. And He sent a river through Eden to water the garden.

Then the Lord called the man Adam and commanded him: "You may eat the fruit of every tree in the garden. But you must not eat the fruit on the tree of life or on the tree of knowledge. The day you eat the fruit on those trees you shall surely die."

God also said, "It is not good that this man should be alone." So He brought Adam all the living creatures He had made, and Adam named them. But still he did not have a companion.

God caused a deep sleep to fall on Adam. Then He took one of Adam's ribs. He closed up Adam's side and from the rib made a woman and brought her to Adam. And they were man and wife.

In the garden there was a serpent. One day he said to Eve, "Has God said that you shall not eat of every tree in the garden?"

Eve answered, "We may eat the fruit of the trees, but we must neither eat nor touch the fruit of the tree in the midst of the garden. God has said, 'You shall not eat it, neither shall you touch it, lest you die.'"

The serpent said, "You will not die. For God knows that the day you eat that fruit, your eyes shall be opened and you will be like gods, knowing good and evil."

When Eve saw that the tree bore fruit which was good for food, and that to eat of it would make her wise, she took some and ate it. She also gave some to Adam and he ate it. Immediately, Eve and her husband knew they had done wrong, and they were ashamed. They sewed fig leaves together to make clothes to cover themselves.

In the cool of the day God walked through the garden. Adam and Eve hid themselves among the trees, but God called to Adam, "Where are you?"

Adam answered, "We heard your voice in the garden and hid because we were afraid."

Then God knew what they had done and was angry.

He placed a curse on the serpent, saying, "The rest of your life you shall crawl in the dust. There will be hatred between you and people walking. They shall crush your head, and you will bruise their heel."

To Adam and Eve, God said, "Because you did not obey Me, you shall live in sorrow. You will work and suffer until you die."

Then God made coats of skins and clothed them and sent them out of the garden of Eden, lest they eat also of the tree of life and live forever. At the entrance He placed angels and a flaming sword which turned in every direction, to guard the tree of life.

Cain and His Brother Abel

ADAM AND EVE HAD TWO SONS, CAIN AND Abel. Cain was a tiller of the ground and Abel was a keeper of sheep. Cain and Abel made offerings to the Lord. Cain brought the fruit of the earth and Abel brought one of his first lambs.

The Lord respected Abel's offering, but did not like Cain's. Cain was very disappointed and angry. One day soon after, out in the fields, Cain killed Abel, because he was jealous.

The Lord said to Cain, "Where is Abel, your brother?"

Cain answered, "I do not know. Am I my brother's keeper?"

Then the Lord said, "What have you done? You have killed your brother, and his blood cries to Me from the ground. From now on you will continue to till the soil, but with poor results. You shall be a fugitive and a wanderer on the earth."

Cain pleaded with the Lord, "My punishment is greater than I can bear. Nevermore shall I see Your face. I shall be a fugitive, and everyone who comes upon me will want to kill me."

Therefore the Lord set a mark upon Cain, so that no one should kill him, and Cain went away from the land of Eden.

Some years later, Adam and Eve had another son whom they called Seth, and he replaced Abel, whom Cain had killed.

Noah's Ark

IT CAME TO PASS THAT, WHEN MEN MULTI- plied and spread over the earth, God looked at them and found that there was much wickedness among them. He was sorry He had created man and decided to destroy

him—not only man, but all living things, beasts, creeping things, and the fowls of the air.

But there was one man named Noah, a descendant of Seth, whom God found good. Noah was a just man and led a good life. One day God said to him, "I will bring a flood of waters to destroy all living things upon the earth, for it is filled with wickedness. Build an ark of gopher wood, three stories high. Divide it into rooms; put a window in the top and a door in the side. Cover it well with pitch to keep out the water.

"Then go into the ark and take with you your wife, your sons, Shem, Ham, and Japheth, and their wives. Take a pair of every sort of living animal into the ark to keep them alive with you, and also enough food for you and for them."

Noah did as God told him, and then the rain began. For forty days and forty nights it fell, until all the mountains were covered and every living thing had been destroyed. Only Noah, and all those that were with him in the ark, remained alive.

For one hundred and fifty days the waters covered the earth. Then God made a wind pass over the earth, and the waters began to recede. On the seventeenth day of the seventh month, the ark came to rest on Mt. Ararat.

Noah let loose a raven, which flew about and did not return, and also a dove, which could find no place to rest and so came back. Noah waited seven more days and again let the dove fly out. That evening the bird returned with an olive leaf in her mouth, so Noah knew that the waters were drying and that trees were growing again.

In another month they went out from the ark, for the land was dry at last. They were joyful and offered praise and thanksgiving to God. The animals set out for the forests and plains, and Noah and his sons went forth to build new homes.

God blessed Noah and his sons and made them a promise: that while the earth remained, there should be seed-time and harvest, cold and heat, summer and winter, and day and night. And He set a rainbow to be in the clouds when it rained, to remind Noah and his descendants that the waters should no more become a flood to destroy the earth.

The Tower of Babel

THE FAMILIES OF THE SONS OF NOAH GREW into nations, all speaking the same language.

As they journeyed from the east, they found a plain in the land of Shinar and dwelt there. They said to one another, "Let us build a city, and in the city a tower whose top may reach to heaven. Let us also choose a name for ourselves, lest we be scattered over the whole earth and be separated."

They set to making bricks, and they cemented them together with mud for mortar. They hoped the tower would last forever.

The Lord came down to see the city and the tower which the children of men were building, and He said, "Behold! these people are one, and speak the same language. They begin to feel that they can accomplish anything they desire. I shall confound their language so that they may not understand one another's speech."

No longer able to talk together, the people left off building their city and their tower, which they called "Babel" because it was confusing.

From Babel they scattered abroad over the face of all the earth, forming different nations with different languages.

Abraham

NOAH HAD MANY DESCENDANTS. IN THE tenth generation of the family of Shem, three sons were born to Terah, who dwelt in the land of Ur. They were named Abraham and Nahor and Haran.

After the death of his youngest son, Terah left his home. He took with him Abraham and his wife, Sarah, and Lot, Haran's son. Leaving behind Nahor and his wife, Milcah, they went forth to settle in the land of Haran. There they lived until the death of Terah, many years later.

Soon after the death of Terah, the Lord appeared to Abraham and said, "Leave your father's house and country. I will show you a new land where you are to go. There a great nation will spring from you, and your name shall be great. In you all the families of the earth shall be blessed."

Abraham took his wife, Sarah, and his nephew, Lot—now a grown man—and all their belongings and followers. They departed from Haran and traveled down toward the land of Canaan.

On the way, the herdsmen of Lot and Abraham quarreled over which should have the better grazing land for his flocks. Therefore, Abraham said to Lot, "Let there be no strife between us, for we are brethren. The whole land is before us. Choose in which direction you will go and let us separate in peace."

Lot chose to settle near by on the plains of Jordan, which were well-watered and fertile. So they separated, and Lot dwelt in the city of Sodom, which was a very wicked city, while Abraham continued on toward the land of Canaan.

The Destruction of Sodom and Gomorrah

IT CAME TO PASS THAT GOD GREW ANGRY at the wickedness of Sodom and the neighboring cities of the plain. He sent down two angels disguised as men to see if there were any good people living there, for God planned to destroy the cities.

As the angels entered the gates of Sodom, Lot was sitting where they passed. Seeing that they were strangers and that it was late, Lot offered them food and shelter in his house for the night.

Before they had gone to bed, some men of the city came knocking at Lot's door. They wanted to see the strangers and abuse them. When Lot refused to let them in, they started to break down his door. The angels drew Lot indoors and struck the men blind. They could no longer find the door, so they went away.

When morning came, the angels warned Lot to hasten away with his wife and daughters, for they had found no other good people in the city. They warned them to walk straight ahead and not so much as turn their heads toward the wicked cities, lest evil befall them.

Then the Lord rained fire and brimstone on Sodom and Gomorrah. He laid waste the cities and all the plain and all the inhabitants. As Lot and his family fled, Lot's wife did not heed the warning of the Lord. She turned to look back, and was instantly changed to a pillar of salt. But Lot and his daughters went up into the mountains and dwelt near the city of Zoar.

The Testing of Abraham

AFTER LEAVING LOT, ABRAHAM HAD BEEN moving from one place to another, for the land of Canaan was then inhabited by the Hittites, and Abraham possessed no land of his own.

One evening, before the ruin of Sodom and Gomorrah, he had fallen into a deep sleep, in which the Lord appeared.

"Know surely," said the Lord, "that I have given this land to your descendants. First they shall be strangers in a land that is not theirs, and for four hundred years they shall serve the people in that land. But the day will come when they shall be freed, and they shall possess the land of Canaan, from the river of Egypt up to the great river Euphrates."

Abraham did not understand how the land could belong to his descendants, for Sarah had had no children. But soon after the Lord had spoken to Abraham, Sarah gave birth to a baby boy, whom they named Isaac. They loved him very dearly, for he was the child of their old age.

When Isaac was a young lad, God made a test of Abraham to see if he would really obey all of His commands, He appeared before Abraham and said, "Take your son, Isaac, whom you love so well, and offer him as a burnt offering to Me on a mountain which I will show you."

Abraham made ready to obey at once, and in the morning he rose early, split wood to make the fire, loaded it on his ass, and with Isaac and two of his young men set off for the mountain. They traveled for three days, and then Abraham saw the place which God had indicated. He turned to his young men and said, "Stay here with the ass while Isaac and I go up on the mountain to worship."

They went up the mountain. There Abraham built an altar and started to arrange the wood for the fire. Then Isaac asked, "Father, where is the lamb for the burnt offering? You have here only the fire and the wood."

Abraham answered sadly, "My son, God Himself will provide the lamb." Then he bound Isaac and laid him on the wood. Stretching out his hand for his knife, Abraham was just about to kill his son when God sent an angel to stop him.

"Abraham! Abraham!" the angel called. "God sees that you were willing to sacrifice your only son. He knows that you fear Him and love Him well. Do not lay your hand on the boy."

Abraham looked round when he heard the voice, and there, to his great joy, he saw a ram in a thicket. He took the ram and offered him as a burnt sacrifice instead of his son.

Then God sent his angel down a second time to say to Abraham, "Because you did not withhold your only son whom you love so well, because you obeyed my command, I will bless you. Your children shall have many children and your descendants shall spread throughout the earth and be blessed."

Joyfully Abraham and Isaac went down to the young men and returned home.

Rebecca at the Well

ABRAHAM BECAME A GREAT MAN. HE HAD many flocks, and herds, much silver and gold, many servants and camels and asses, but still he owned no land.

When Sarah died, Abraham had no place to bury her, so he determined to buy some land at once. The Hittites offered him space in their choicest cemeteries, but Abraham wanted land that he could call his own. He bought a cave from a man named Ephron, and Ephron gave him also the field about the cave, and the trees. They fixed the boundaries so that the land belonged to Abraham, and Sarah was buried there.

Abraham and his son Isaac mourned over the death of Sarah. And Abraham was worried because Isaac was not yet married, although he was now a fine young man, and one day would inherit a great fortune.

At that time, it was the custom for parents to choose husbands and wives for their children, but Abraham felt that

he was too old to go out in search of a wife for his son. He called to his side an old and trusted servant and spoke to him: "I do not wish Isaac to marry a girl from Canaan. Go back to the country from which we came and find him a wife."

So the servant took ten camels and servants, money and costly gifts, and set out for Haran.

When he neared the city he stopped by the well outside the walls to water his camels. It was early evening, the time when the women went out to draw water. There by the well, the faithful servant prayed to the Lord, "Oh, Lord God, I pray You, give me a sign to help me. When the daughters of the city come out to draw water, I shall ask that one let down her pitcher that I may drink. Let there be one who shall say, 'Drink, and I will give your camels water to drink also.' Let that same girl be the one You have chosen for Your servant Isaac."

Even before he had done speaking, there came a very beautiful girl, Rebecca, with her pitcher upon her shoulder. When she had filled her pitcher, the servant asked for a drink. Graciously, she let down her pitcher from her shoulder, and gave him a drink. And when he had finished, she drew water and filled the trough for all his camels to drink. The servant, knowing that the Lord was guiding him, asked her name. When she said, "Rebecca, daughter of Bethuel, son of Milcah, who was the wife of Abraham's brother Nahor," he bowed his head and thanked the Lord. Then he went with Rebecca to call upon her family.

To her mother and her brother, Laban, the man explained his errand. He told of Abraham's wealth and age, and of his desire to find a girl of his own tribe as a wife for his only son. He told them also of his prayer asking the Lord to give him a sign, and said that Rebecca had been chosen.

The servant asked that Rebecca be allowed to return with him to be Isaac's wife. The girl's family agreed, and they prepared a great feast. Abraham's servant brought forth the jewels and gifts Abraham had sent for Rebecca. He also gave precious gifts to her mother and brother. After a day of feasting, they said farewell to Rebecca and she departed with Abraham's servant and his men.

One evening, while Isaac was out in the field, he saw the camels coming in the distance, and he went to meet them. The servant told all that had passed, how young and beautiful Rebecca was, and how kind she had been.

So Isaac and Rebecca were married and were very happy with each other. Abraham was pleased to see that his son had married such a good wife, and he gave all he possessed to Isaac. He died in peace at a good old age, and Isaac buried him in the cave beside his wife, Sarah.

Esau and Jacob

ISAAC AND REBECCA HAD TWIN SONS, WHOM they named Esau and Jacob. As the boys grew older, they were quite different, not only in appearance but also in temperament. Esau, the first-born, was a very fine hunter and a man of the fields. Jacob was more quiet, a plain man who dwelt in the tents. Isaac preferred Esau because Isaac, too, loved the outdoors, enjoyed hunting, and liked to eat of the venison he had killed. Rebecca's favorite was Jacob, who was quiet and home-loving.

One day, when Jacob was fixing some lentil soup, Esau came in from the field faint and weak from hunger. He asked Jacob for some soup to sustain him. When Jacob saw how weak his brother was, he did not feed him at once, but said, "Sell me first your birthright, so that I may be as the elder son." He would not give Esau any food until he agreed and sold his birthright. Then Jacob gave Esau bread and soup to eat.

The Stolen Blessing

WHEN ISAAC GREW OLD, HE WAS NEARLY blind. Feeling that he would not live much longer, he called his beloved Esau one day and said, "Take your bow and arrows, go out in the woods, and hunt some venison. Then roast it as I like it and bring it to me, so that I may eat it and bless you before I die."

Rebecca heard Isaac, and immediately she wanted his last blessing to be for Jacob, who was her favorite. As soon as Esau was gone to hunt, she sent Jacob to bring her two kids from the flocks, and she prepared the savory meat, roasted as Isaac loved it, and had Jacob bring it to him.

When Jacob brought the food to his father's bedside, he said, "I am Esau, your first-born son. I have done as you said. Sit up and eat, and then bless me."

Isaac, thinking he recognized the voice as Jacob's, asked, "How did you find it so quickly?"

And Jacob answered, "Because the Lord brought it to me."

Isaac, still doubting, said, "Come near that I may feel you and know whether or not you are really Esau."

Rebecca had already thought of this. Not only had she dressed Jacob in Esau's clothes, but she had covered his smooth hands and arms with the skins of the lambs, so that they were very hairy, like Esau's. Isaac felt his hands, since he could not see, and said, "The voice is the voice of Jacob, but the hands are the hands of Esau."

Then he ate the meat and bread and drank the wine that Jacob had brought him. When he had finished, he kissed Jacob and, smelling his raiment, said, "The smell of my son is like the smell of a field which the Lord has blessed. Therefore, God give you rain from heaven, and the richness of the earth, and plenty of corn and wine. You shall be a leader of men and nations."

Jacob had scarcely left his father when Esau came in from his hunting. He also had prepared savory meat and brought it to his father.

"Who are you?" Isaac asked.

Esau answered, "I am your son, your first-born, Esau."

Isaac, trembling, asked, "Where is the one who just brought me venison? I ate it all before you came, and I blessed him."

When Esau heard this, he cried out bitterly, "Bless me,

too, father. For it is Jacob who tricked you to get your blessing. First he took away my birthright, and now he has stolen your last blessing. Oh, father, have you not one for me?"

Isaac answered sadly, "I have already made Jacob lord of the family and promised him wealth. That I cannot change. You shall serve your brother, but the time will come when you will be free."

From that day on, Esau hated his brother. He vowed that when his father should die and the days of mourning should be over, he would slay his brother, Jacob.

When Rebecca heard of this, she called Jacob and told him, "Your brother intends to kill you. Therefore, once more do as I tell you. Go to my brother Laban in Haran, and stay with him awhile until Esau's anger has passed and he forgets what you have done. Then I will send for you."

In order to obtain Isaac's permission for Jacob to go, Rebecca said, "It is enough that Esau has married a Hittite girl. If Jacob does the same, we shall have lost all connection with my tribe. He must find a wife in Haran."

Isaac agreed, as Rebecca knew he would. He called Jacob and charged him, saying, "Do not take for a wife a daughter of the land of Canaan. Go to your mother's people and find a wife there. May God bless you and give you many children. May you inherit the land where you are a stranger, the land which God promised to the descendants of Abraham."

With this blessing, Jacob set out for Haran.

Jacob's Ladder

ONE NIGHT DURING HIS JOURNEY TO Haran, Jacob stopped by the wayside to rest, and there he dreamed a very wonderful dream. He saw before him a golden ladder set upon the earth. The top of it reached to heaven, and the angels of God were ascending and descending on it. At the very top, above them all, stood the Lord, who spoke to him, "I am the Lord, God of Abraham and of Isaac. The land upon which you are lying now I will give to you and your children. And they shall spread over the land in all directions and be blessed. No matter where you wander, I shall be with you and bring you back one day. For I shall not leave you until this is done."

Jacob awoke with a start. He was a little afraid, for he felt he had been at the very gates of heaven. He rose early in the morning, gathered a few stones, made a pillar and poured oil over it. And he called the place Bethel, which means the "house of God."

Rachel and Leah

JACOB CONTINUED ON HIS JOURNEY UNTIL he came to Laban's house in Haran. There Jacob lived with his uncle, helping with the cattle and goats.

At the end of a month, Laban spoke to him: "Because you are my nephew, you should not be expected to contribute your labor for nothing. What wages shall I pay you?"

Jacob, who loved Rachel, Laban's younger daughter, said he would work for seven years if Rachel could then become his wife. Laban agreed, and Jacob worked for seven years, caring for his uncle's herds and flocks. At the end of that time, Laban refused to let him marry Rachel, but gave him instead his older daughter, Leah.

Jacob was very unhappy, for he loved Rachel and did not love Leah. So Laban agreed to give him Rachel for a wife, too, if he would stay and work for another seven years.

Leah bore Jacob six sons and daughters before Rachel had any children. When Rachel's first baby was born, he was called Joseph, and Jacob loved him more than all the others, for he was Rachel's son.

After Joseph's birth, Jacob wanted to leave the land of Haran and go back to Canaan. But each time he mentioned it to his uncle, Laban promised him better wages, cattle and goats for himself, if he would stay. So gradually, Jacob acquired herds and flocks of his own, and camels and servants.

Laban's sons, who were not so successful as Jacob, began to protest to their father, and the families were not happy together. Then one night, an angel of God appeared to Jacob in a dream, and told him to go back to Canaan.

Jacob's Homecoming

ONE DAY, WHEN LABAN HAD GONE OFF TO the fields to shear his sheep, Jacob gathered all the flocks and herds which Laban had promised him. He set his wives and children on camels, and without saying anything to his uncle, he departed.

When Laban returned after three days, and saw what had happened, he summoned his sons and servants and set out after Jacob, intending to bring him back. For Jacob was a good worker and very successful with the animals. But before he overtook Jacob, God warned Laban to do him no harm.

When, after seven days' journey, he did come up to Jacob's caravan, he was very angry and quarreled with Jacob. But Jacob answered, "For twenty years I have worked for you. I have guarded your flocks day and night,

The brothers seized Joseph and cast him into a deep pit. (Page 28)

When the brothers arrived in Egypt, they bowed down before the governor.
(Page 33)

in heat and bitter cold, and always replaced any sheep that were missing or killed. Unless you knew that God were with me, you would have sent me back to Canaan empty-handed. I have taken with me only what I earned."

Laban, knowing this was true, protested his friendship for Jacob, blessed his daughters and their children, and returned to his home.

Jacob and his family continued on their way until they approached the land of Edom, through which they had to pass. Jacob's brother, Esau, had settled in Edom, and he too was now wealthy and had great flocks and herds and many servants.

Jacob was afraid, for even after all these years he remembered how he had cheated his brother, and that Esau had vowed to kill him. Thinking to soften his brother's heart, he sent ahead servants with rich presents for Esau, more than two hundred goats and lambs, camels, cattle and bulls and asses.

That night, God appeared again to Jacob and told him that his name should be called Israel, because he had power from God, and that his descendants and their tribes would be called the children of Israel.

In the morning, Jacob saw Esau coming toward him with four hundred men. Fearful, he stepped out in front of everyone and bowed himself to the ground seven times before his brother. Esau ran to meet him, and kissed him and wept. He was no longer bitter or angry, and long ago had forgiven Jacob. Jacob learned that his father, Isaac, was still living, but that Rebecca, his mother, had died.

Esau and Jacob parted in peace, and Jacob and his family went on to Canaan.

As they were passing Bethel, where Jacob years before had had his dream on the way to Haran, Rachel gave birth to her second baby. She called him Benoni, "son of my sorrow," for she knew that her end had come. And afterward she died. But sad as he was over Rachel's death, Jacob could not give her son such a name, so he called him Benjamin, "son of my right hand." Joseph and Benjamin, Rachel's two boys, were his best-loved children.

Soon after Jacob arrived in Canaan, Isaac died. Esau came from Edom, and the two brothers buried their father. And Jacob, in fulfillment of his father's last prayer and blessing, settled in the land of Canaan, where once, long ago, his grandfather Abraham had been a stranger.

Joseph and the Coat of Many Colors

JACOB LIVED IN THE LAND OF CANAAN WITH his twelve sons. He was a rich man, and owned great flocks of sheep and goats, and herds of cattle. The ten eldest sons tended the flocks. The eleventh son, Joseph, his father's favorite, and the youngest son, Benjamin, remained at home with their father.

Jacob showed in many ways how much he loved Joseph. On Joseph's seventeenth birthday, his father gave him a beautiful coat of many colors. When his older brothers saw it, they were jealous and angry. They hated Joseph and could not speak kindly to him.

At about the same time, Joseph had a strange dream, that he and his brothers were binding sheaves of wheat in the field. His sheaf stood upright while his brothers' sheaves bowed down before it. When Joseph told his brothers of this dream, they became very angry and hated him even more, for to them it meant that he, their younger brother, would rule over them.

And then Joseph told of yet another dream in which the sun, the moon, and eleven stars bowed before him. This time even his father rebuked him, saying, "What is this dream? Shall I and your mother and brothers bow down before you?" The older brothers made no effort to conceal their anger against the lad.

One day, when the older brothers had taken the flocks to the rich grazing fields in Shechem, some distance away, Jacob sent Joseph to see if all were well and to bring back news of them. It took Joseph a long time to reach them, for they had moved on further to Dothan.

As he approached, his brothers saw the beautiful coat in the distance. Realizing that it was Joseph, alone, they saw a chance to be rid of him and his dreams. They talked among themselves and decided to kill him, to throw him into a near-by pit and say that a wild beast had devoured him.

The eldest brother, Reuben, persuaded them that it would be better not to shed any blood, but to throw him into the pit and leave him there in the wilderness. He secretly planned to return later and rescue Joseph from the pit, and to return him to Jacob.

When Joseph came up to his brothers, they seized him, tore off his coat of many colors, and cast him into a deep pit from which he could not escape.

Reuben went away to tend the flocks, and the other brothers sat down to eat. Just then a camel caravan of Ishmaelite merchants came passing by, on their way to trade in Egypt. One of the brothers, Judah, suggested that they sell Joseph as a slave and thus make some money for themselves, rather than kill him or leave him in the pit; for, after all, he was their brother. So they lifted Joseph from the pit and sold him to the merchants for twenty pieces of silver.

When Reuben returned and found Joseph gone, he was filled with despair, fearing that in his absence the others had killed him. But when he learned that Joseph was alive and had been sold as a slave, he fell in with the plan of his brothers. They killed one of the goats and dipped Joseph's coat in its blood. When they returned home, they showed the coat to Jacob.

"We found this coat," they said. "Do you know if it is Joseph's?"

Poor Jacob recognized the coat and, beholding it torn and bloody, cried out that some evil beast must have attacked and killed his favorite son. Jacob put on sackcloth and mourned for Joseph, and all his other sons could not comfort him. He could only weep and declare, "I will go to my grave mourning for my son."

Joseph in Prison

WHEN THE ISHMAELITE MERCHANTS brought Joseph to Egypt, they sold him as a slave to Potiphar, who was a captain of the guard in the palace of the Pharaoh, ruler of Egypt.

Joseph was a good youth and guided by the Lord. He served Potiphar well, so Potiphar made him manager of his house and fields. But when Potiphar's wife, who was jealous of Joseph, accused him of something he did not do, Joseph was cast into prison. Still the Lord was with Joseph, and the keeper of the prison favored him. He was given charge of some of the prisoners and then of all, and under his supervision life among the prisoners became more bearable.

In the prison at the same time with Joseph were two servants of Pharaoh, his chief butler and his chief baker. Joseph noticed one morning that they seemed worried. When he asked the reason, the two men told him that they had dreamed strange dreams which they could not understand. They told their dreams to Joseph.

The chief butler said, "I dreamed there was a vine before me. It had three branches that budded, blossomed, and brought forth ripe grapes. I pressed the grapes into Pharaoh's cup and gave it to him."

Joseph said to him, "The three branches are three days. Within three days Pharaoh will release you from prison and you shall give him his cup as you did when you were his butler. When things go well with you, remember me and speak of me to Pharaoh so that I may be freed from this prison."

The baker had dreamed that he was carrying three baskets of pastry for Pharaoh, and that three birds came and ate the cakes from the top basket. Joseph said, "The three baskets are three days. Within three days the Pharaoh shall have you hanged on a tree and the birds shall eat your flesh."

Three days later, which was the Pharaoh's birthday, the

king prepared a feast for all his servants. The chief baker was hanged, but the chief butler was restored to his former position. As soon as he was free, however, the butler forgot all about Joseph.

For two years Joseph remained in the jail. And then one night Pharaoh had a strange dream. He told his magicians and they could not interpret it. He called all the wise men in Egypt, but none of them could help him. Only then did the chief butler remember Joseph, and that his own dream had turned out as Joseph had foretold. He told Pharaoh, who ordered Joseph to be brought to him. Joseph was then hastily taken out of the prison, bathed and shaved, and given fresh clothes. Then he was brought before Pharaoh, who informed him of his strange dream.

"In my dream I stood on the bank of a river and saw seven fat cows come up out of the water to feed in a meadow. Seven other cows came up after them—poor, lean cows such as I have never seen in Egypt. These lean cows ate up the first seven fat ones, but they were still as thin as if they had eaten nothing. So I awoke.

"I slept again and dreamed a second time that seven ears of corn came up on one stalk—healthy and good. And seven withered and thin ears came up after them and devoured them. I have told this to the magicians, but no one can declare the meaning of these dreams."

Joseph said to Pharaoh, "In your dream, God is showing

you what He is about to do. The seven good cows and the seven good ears are seven years of great plenty throughout the land of Egypt. The seven lean cows and the seven thin ears are seven years of famine that shall follow. All the plenty shall be gone and forgotten. The famine will be great and will consume the land. God has sent you the same dream twice to show you how grievous it will be and to say these things will happen soon."

Therefore, Joseph told Pharaoh, he should soon choose a wise man to rule over the land of Egypt. This man should appoint officers over all the land who would see that one fifth of all the food and corn planted during the seven plenteous years should be gathered and stored in the cities, under Pharaoh's seal. Then, when the seven years of famine should follow, the land of Egypt still would not want for food.

Joseph as Governor of Egypt

JOSEPH'S WORDS SEEMED VERY WISE TO PHAraoh and his servants, so the king said to Joseph, "Since God has shown all of this to you, you shall rule over my house and my people. Only on the throne shall I be greater than you."

And Pharaoh took off his ring and put it on Joseph's

hand. He clothed him in fine linen, put a gold chain around his neck, and gave him his second chariot.

Joseph, then thirty years old, went throughout all the land of Egypt. In the seven plenteous years he saw that food and grain were gathered and stored equally in all the cities. Then came the famine over all the face of the earth. But in Egypt there was food. When the Egyptians were famished and cried out for bread, Pharaoh sent them to Joseph, for he was the governor of Egypt and had charge of all the royal storehouses. Joseph opened the storehouses and sold the people food. And people of all countries came to Egypt to buy corn, because in no other land had grain been stored for the years of famine.

Meanwhile, in the land of Canaan, Joseph's father and brothers and their families suffered greatly from the famine. When Jacob heard that there was grain in Egypt, he said to his sons, "Go down to Egypt and buy grain for us that we may live and not die of hunger." So the ten older brothers went to buy corn in Egypt. Jacob kept Benjamin at home, for fear something might happen to the lad he loved, even as it had happened to his beloved Joseph.

When the brothers arrived in Egypt and presented themselves to the governor, they bowed down before him, just as it had been foretold in Joseph's dream of the sheaves of wheat. Joseph recognized his brothers at once, but they did not know him, for he had been only a young lad when they had sold him into slavery. To test them, Joseph accused them of being spies, come to see how bad the famine was in Egypt.

They answered, "No, we are twelve brothers, the sons of Jacob of Canaan. Our youngest brother is at home with his father and the other is dead." But Joseph, still pretending to believe they were spies, refused to let them go unless their youngest brother were brought before him.

"Send one of you to fetch your brother. The rest of you I shall keep here in prison until your words are proved true." Then he had them all put in jail.

At the end of three days, Joseph called them before him and said, "Do this, for I fear God. If you be true men, let one of you stay here while the others carry corn to allay the famine of your families. But make sure you bring back your youngest brother to me to prove your words are not false."

The brothers, fearing that this trouble had come to them as punishment for the way they had treated their younger brother years before, did not dare to disobey. They left Simeon in prison and started on the journey back to Canaan with their sacks full of corn.

They stopped overnight at an inn. One of them opened a sack for grain to feed his ass, and found in the top the money he had paid the Egyptian governor. This the brothers could not understand, for they did not yet know that Joseph had ordered their money to be given back in each sack of corn.

Upon their return, they related to their father all that had befallen them. Then as they emptied their sacks, and each found his bundle of money, they were afraid. Then Jacob refused to let them take Benjamin back to Egypt. Joseph, his favorite, had been lost long ago, and now Simeon was in prison. He wanted nothing more to befall his sons.

After a time, when they had eaten all the grain they had brought from Egypt, and there was still famine in the land, Jacob said to his sons, "Go again, and buy us some food."

But Judah answered, "The governor of Egypt will not even see us unless we bring our brother. Send him with me, that we and our families, and he, too, shall not starve."

Jacob finally agreed and had them take presents to the governor: fruits, balm, honey, spices, nuts, and myrrh. And he had them take double the amount of money that had been returned in their sacks. Then, with Benjamin, the brothers set forth for Egypt.

When the steward brought the news that the nine strangers had returned with their younger brother, Joseph ordered them to be brought to his house. The brothers, now more frightened than ever that they should all be taken as slaves, explained to the steward how they had found the money in their sacks and had brought back double the amount to return it and to buy more grain. The steward answered, "Peace! Fear not. It was God's will that I return your money," and he brought Simeon to them. He gave them water to wash their feet before entering Joseph's house, and gave them food for their beasts.

They made themselves ready, and when they came before Joseph, they gave him the presents which Jacob had sent. Then they were seated at a separate table, for the Hebrews and the Egyptians did not eat together, and Joseph sent them food, giving more to Benjamin than to all the others. And they ate and drank and were merry with him. Then Joseph commanded his steward to fill their sacks with grain, as much as they could carry, to return their money as before, and to put into Benjamin's sack Joseph's own silver cup.

The next morning, soon after the brothers had left, Joseph told his steward to follow them. When the steward caught up with them and accused them of stealing his master's cup, they all denied it, and agreed that if it were found, the one in whose sack it was concealed must return as Joseph's servant. When it was found in Benjamin's sack, the brothers were terribly frightened and all returned to Joseph.

They bowed to the ground before him and pleaded with him not to keep Benjamin, for it would break their father's heart. Judah spoke up, "Our father is an old man and this

Pharaoh's daughter was astonished to see a baby in the basket. (Page 40)

Moses saw a bush in flames, but not burned away. (Page 41)

is his youngest son. I swore to him that I would bring this boy back safely, that no harm should befall him. Keep me instead to be your servant, and let the lad go with his brothers."

At this point Joseph was overcome with emotion. He sent away all his servants, and weeping, called his brothers near to him.

"I am Joseph," he told them, "your brother, whom you sold into Egypt." The brothers were greatly troubled and could not speak a word. Seeing this, Joseph continued, "Do not grieve or be angry with yourselves for having sold me. God sent me here before you to save your lives. For two years there has been famine in Egypt. There are yet five years more. It was not you, but God, that sent me here and made me lord and ruler of the Pharaoh's house and land.

"Hasten—go to my father and tell him that his son Joseph bids him come to Egypt. And come you, with your families and herds, so that you may survive the famine." And he kissed his brothers, and forgave them, and sent them home to Jacob, their asses laden with grain, with meat and bread and clothes for the journey.

When Jacob heard the news he could not believe it. But when the brothers told him all that Joseph had said, he spoke, "It is enough. Joseph is yet alive. I will go to see him before I die."

They gathered all their goods, their families and their

herds, and they traveled to Egypt. Since the brothers were fine herdsmen, the Pharaoh welcomed them and gave them land in Goshen, near by, and made them keepers of all his cattle. Thus Jacob lived near Joseph until the end of his days, and from his twelve sons sprang the twelve tribes of Israel.

Moses
in the Bulrushes

FOR SEVERAL HUNDREDS OF YEARS THE descendants of Jacob's sons lived in Egypt, and in time there were a large number of them in the land. Now a new king ruled over Egypt, one who did not know of Joseph and the good he had done. He saw only that there were a great many Hebrews and that they were growing powerful and rich, so he said to his people, "Behold! these children of Israel are mightier than we. Let us be wise and take action lest they join with our enemies and take our land.''

Therefore he ordered that the Hebrews be made to work at brick-making and building his treasure cities, and he set taskmasters over them to keep them at their work. But the more they were oppressed, the more numerous and the stronger the Hebrews grew. So the Egyptians made slaves of them. They put them to labor with mortar and brick, in the fields, and thus made their lives bitter with hard bondage.

When the Hebrews still continued to multiply and to prosper, the Pharaoh ordered that every male baby born to them should be drowned in the river. He thought that in this way he would soon be rid of them.

One of the Hebrew women had a boy baby. He was such a good and sturdy child that she could not bear to see him drowned. She managed to hide him until he was three months old. Then, fearful that some day an Egyptian might find him and kill him, she devised a plan to try to save him. She built a little basket of bulrushes, daubed it with pitch, put her little son in it, and set it among the reeds by the river's brink. The baby's sister stood near by to see what happened to the child hidden there.

It chanced that the daughter of the Pharaoh came down to the river to wash. Seeing the basket, she sent one of her maidens to fetch it. When she opened it, she was astonished to see a baby inside. The Pharaoh's daughter saw that it was a Hebrew baby, but she had pity on it and decided to keep it. Then the baby's sister came forward and asked, "Shall I get a nurse from the Hebrew women to care for the child?"

This seemed a good idea to the Pharaoh's daughter, so she agreed, and the girl, naturally, fetched her own mother. The King's daughter said, "Take this child away and nurse him for me. I will pay you."

The baby's own mother took care of him until he was a young lad, and then she brought him to the Pharaoh's daughter and he became her son. She called him Moses because she drew him from the water.

When Moses was a grown man, he went among his own people and beheld the hardships under which they were forced to live. One day he saw an Egyptian taskmaster beating one of his people. He looked this way and that, and seeing no one else near, he slew the Egyptian and hid his body in the sand.

When he went out the second day, Moses saw two Hebrews fighting. He said to the man who was in the wrong, "Why do you strike your fellow?" And the Hebrew answered, "Who made *you* ruler over us? Do you intend to kill me as you did the Egyptian?" Moses was thoroughly frightened, for he saw that his deed, committed in anger, already was known.

When the Pharaoh heard of it, he sought to have Moses executed, but Moses escaped and fled from the land. Moses traveled far down the Red Sea into the land of Midian—where he was surely out of all danger from the Egyptians.

One evening, being weary, he sat down to rest at a well by the way.

Now the priest of Midian, Jethro, had seven daughters, who came each evening to this well to draw water for their father's flocks. The shepherds near by often came and drove them away. Moses, seeing this, came to their assistance. When they told their father how kind the stranger had been, he sent for Moses to partake of their hospitality. It came about that Moses stayed on to live with them. Later he married one of the daughters, Zipporah, and took care of Jethro's flocks.

Moses Chosen Leader

THOUGH THE KING OF EGYPT DIED AND another ruled in his place, the Hebrews were still kept in bondage, and they cried out to God for help. God heard their cries, for one day, when Moses had led Jethro's flocks to the mountains to graze, he saw a bush in flames, but not burned away. When he went closer to see why the bush was not burned, God called to him and said, "Moses, I am here. Come no nearer. Take off your shoes, for you are standing on holy ground."

Moses hid his face, for he was afraid to look at God. And the Lord said, "I have seen the affliction of my people in Egypt and have heard their cry. I know their sorrows and I have come down to deliver them from the Egyptians and bring them away to a good land. Come now, and I will send you to the Pharaoh to bring my people, the children of Israel, out of Egypt."

Moses was troubled, for he did not know what he could say to Pharaoh or the Hebrews. But God, seeing this, told him, "To the Hebrews say, 'The Lord God of your fathers, the God of Jacob, has sent me. He has seen your sorrow and will bring you out of the affliction of Egypt into the good land of Canaan—a land flowing with milk and honey.' They will hearken to your voice. Then go—you and the elders of Israel—to the king of Egypt and say to him, 'The Lord God of the Hebrews has told us to go into the wilderness for three days, that we may pray and make sacrifice to Him.' He will not let you go. But then I will stretch out My hand and strike a blow at all Egypt; and after that he will let you go. But when you go, do not go empty-handed."

Moses continued to be afraid that the Hebrews would not believe him. God grew angry and said, "Your brother Aaron will come to meet you. I will be your voice and speak for both of you and will instruct you in what to do. I know that Aaron speaks well, so he will be the spokesman to your people. To you I give this rod, with which you will do wonders that will also serve to convince them."

Moses took his family and returned to Egypt. Aaron came to meet him, and Moses told him all that God had said. Then they gathered together all the elders of the Hebrews, and Aaron told them all the things God had said to Moses. When the leaders heard these things and saw the wonders which Moses did, they believed that the Lord had really spoken with Moses; that He had heard their cries and that they would be saved.

Moses and the Plagues

MOSES AND AARON WENT TO THE PHAraoh and asked that all the Hebrews be allowed to go to pray and make sacrifices to God for three days in the wilderness. But the king refused. Not only that, but because they had been so bold as to ask, he gave orders to the taskmasters to double the work of his Hebrew slaves.

Until this time the brick-makers had been supplied with straw to make their bricks. But now the Pharaoh ordered that they gather the straw themselves and still make as many bricks. On the next day, when some had not found any straw, the slaves were beaten for not having made the usual number of bricks. The Hebrews were discouraged, and complained to Moses and Aaron because conditions were now much worse than before.

The next morning, when the Pharaoh went down to the river, Moses met him there and asked again that his people might be permitted to go. When the Pharaoh refused, Moses struck the river with the rod God had given him. Instantly the waters turned to blood, and all the fish died. The river ran with blood for seven days.

Still Pharaoh refused to let the Hebrews go. Then God sent a plague of frogs to cover the land of Egypt. Greatly disturbed, Pharaoh called Moses and Aaron and said to them, "Beg your Lord to rid us of these frogs, and I will let your people go to pray."

So Moses prayed that God would take away the plague of frogs, and God did. The frogs died in the houses and villages and fields. The people gathered them together in heaps, and the land stank with their rotting bodies. But as soon as the plague was gone, Pharaoh forgot his promise.

Then God sent a plague of lice and then swarms of flies into all the houses. And He made a division between Egypt and the land of Goshen, and none of the plagues touched the Hebrews in Goshen. And then Pharaoh said, "Go! Pray and sacrifice to your God. But do not go out of the country."

Moses insisted they be allowed to go on a three days' journey into the wilderness, away from the Egyptians, and Pharaoh agreed. Moses added, "I will pray to God to remove these plagues. But this time do not deceive us and keep us here after giving us your promise to let us go." And God removed the lice and flies. When they were all gone, again Pharaoh hardened his heart and would not let the people go.

Then the Lord said to Moses, "Go to Pharaoh. Tell him that if he continues to hold you back, tomorrow I will send a plague and all the cattle, the horses, the camels, the oxen and the sheep in Egypt shall die, but none that belong to the Hebrews shall die." And so it came about, but still the Pharaoh would not let the Israelites go.

Moses and Aaron, angry with Pharaoh, went to him with

--◄{ 45 }►--

ashes from the furnace. They stood before him and threw the ashes into the air toward heaven. The ashes became a cloud over the land, and wherever they landed on the Egyptians, they caused boils to break out on the skin. The Pharaoh's magicians were powerless to prevent or cure the boils.

Then Moses warned that he would cause in Egypt a great hailstorm that would kill every living creature which might be caught in it. The Hebrews brought in their cattle and flocks and kept them in their houses and many of the Egyptians who feared the prophecy of Moses did the same. Moses now stretched his rod toward heaven. The Lord sent thunder and fire, and a heavy hail fell throughout all the land of Egypt. It killed all men and beasts that were in the fields, and it broke down all the grain and the branches of the trees. Only in the land of Goshen, where the children of Israel lived, was there no hail.

This time Pharaoh praised the Lord and promised to let the Hebrews go. But when God stopped the hail, Pharaoh saw that many grains had not yet bloomed and so were not completely destroyed, and he would not let the Hebrews go.

Then Moses threatened that God would send a plague of locusts which would cover the earth and eat every growing thing that had not been ruined by the hail. Pharaoh's servants urged him to let the Hebrews go, for their land was being turned into a desert. So Pharaoh called Moses and Aaron and said, "Go and serve the Lord your God. But how many of you want to go?"

Moses said, "All of us, young and old, with our sons and our daughters, with our flocks and our herds. For we must make sacrifices and hold a feast in honor of the Lord."

Pharaoh feared that since Moses wanted everyone to go, they meant to go forever and that the Egyptians thus would lose their valuable laborers. So he agreed to let the men go, but would not permit them to take their children or flocks. Moses, again angered, stretched his rod over the land, and the Lord sent an east wind which brought clouds of locusts. They came so thick that the land and the skies were darkened and they ate every green thing that was to be seen.

Pharaoh begged to be forgiven and pleaded with Moses to take away this terrible plague. God then sent a mighty west wind which blew all the locusts into the Red Sea. But as soon as the land was free of locusts, Pharaoh's heart hardened once more and he would not let the children of Israel go.

Then God sent three days of darkness over Egypt. Only the Hebrews had light in their dwellings; the Egyptians could not see their way about at all. Pharaoh called Moses and said, "You may go, and you may take your children also, but your flocks and herds must stay here."

Moses said, "We must also take our cattle. For we must

offer sacrifices to God, and we do not know what we shall need until we get into the wilderness."

But Pharaoh was angry and said, "Go away from me and let me see your face no more."

And then the Lord said to Moses, "I will bring one last plague upon Pharaoh and upon Egypt, and then he will surely let you go."

The Hebrews made themselves ready, for they knew at last they were about to be set free, and they did all the things which God had commanded.

It was on the fourteenth day of the month, and each family was instructed to slaughter a small lamb. They took a bunch of hyssop, dipped it in the blood of the lamb, and sprinkled the two sideposts and the lintel of each doorway so as to mark their houses. Then they roasted the lamb and ate it with unleavened bread and bitter herbs. None of them went out, but when evening came they ate in haste, fully dressed, even with their staffs in hand. This feast was called the Passover, to signify that the Lord passed over the houses of the Hebrews when He brought the last plague to Egypt.

At midnight, the Lord killed every first-born child in Egypt, from Pharaoh's down to the first-born of the humblest prisoner in the dungeon, and even the first-born of the cattle.

Pharaoh arose in the night with all his servants and all

the Egyptians. Loud was their lamentation, for there was not a house where death had not struck. Pharaoh sent his messengers to the Hebrews, saying, "Go from our land, you and your children. Take your flocks and your herds as you have asked and be gone." And the Egyptian people urged them to go before they should all be dead. In their anxiety to see the Hebrews gone, they heaped on them presents of gold and silver, jewels and clothing.

Thus, after four hundred and thirty years in Egypt, the Hebrews left the land, about six hundred thousand men with women and children, and also with great herds and flocks. And Moses took the bones of Joseph with him.

Thus the Lord brought the children of Israel out of the land of Egypt.

The Escape from Egypt

BY DAY GOD WENT BEFORE THE HEBREWS in a pillar of cloud and by night in a pillar of fire to give them light, and He led them through the wilderness to the Red Sea, where they camped to rest.

When the king of Egypt suddenly realized that all the Hebrews had gone, he and his people asked themselves, "Why have we let these slaves go?" And Pharaoh ordered six hundred chariots to pursue the Hebrews and bring them back.

When the Hebrews saw the Egyptians coming, they cried out to Moses, "Why did you not let us alone? It would have been better to serve the Egyptians than to die here in the wilderness." Moses told his people not to fear, for God would save them. Then the pillar of cloud moved behind them and came between them and the Egyptians, so that the Egyptians could not find them.

Moses stretched out his rod over the sea, and God caused a strong east wind to blow all that night. In the morning the waters were divided, and the Hebrews passed safely over the dry ground between the walls of water on their right and left.

The Egyptians pursued and went in after them. But the chariot wheels of Pharaoh's soldiers first stuck and then came off. The Egyptians were frightened, since they saw that the Hebrews had crossed to the other shore. As the soldiers turned to flee, Moses stretched forth his hand and the Lord caused the waters to rush together again. The chariots and horsemen and all of Pharaoh's army were drowned.

The children of Israel stood on dry ground on the other side—and they feared the Lord and believed in Him and in His servant Moses.

In the Wilderness

MOSES LED THE HEBREWS THROUGH TO the wilderness of Zin. There, during the second month of their journey, their food gave out and they could find no more. Then they cried out against Moses and wished they were back in Egypt, where at least they had had food. The Lord, hearing their complaints, appeared before Moses and said: "I have heard the murmurings of the children of Israel. Say to them, 'This evening you shall eat flesh, and in the morning you shall eat bread. And you shall know that the Lord is your God.'"

That evening flocks of quail swarmed about the camp, and the Hebrews killed them for meat. The next morning the ground was covered with dew. And when the dew had lifted, there remained small white wafers on the ground. When the Hebrews saw it they called it "manna"—for they knew not what it was. They gathered it, and they all ate it. It was there every morning, and each one gathered just what he needed for that day. On the sixth day, before the Sabbath, they gathered enough for two days. So the people rested on the seventh day.

Journeying on through the wilderness, the Children of Israel came to the desert of Zin and pitched their tents there by the oasis of Kadesh. (Moses' sister, Miriam, died and was buried there with honor.) Within a short time there was a scarcity of drinking water. Again the people cried out against Moses and Aaron for having led them out of Egypt, and were ready to stone them because they feared that they might all die of thirst.

Once more the Lord appeared to Moses, saying, "Take the rod, you and your brother Aaron, gather the people together, and speak to the rock in My name before their eyes. It shall give forth water for them and their beasts to drink."

Moses took the rod, as he was commanded, and he and Aaron gathered the people before the rock. In his anger at the Hebrews for doubting, Moses cried out, "Hear now, you rebels! Must we fetch you water out of this rock?" He struck the rock twice, and water came out abundantly, so that the people and their beasts had plenty to drink.

Then the Lord spoke to Moses and Aaron, "Because you did not sanctify Me in the eyes of the children of Israel, and because you did not show them it was the Lord Who brought water from the rock, therefore you shall not live to bring my people into the Promised Land."

The Commandments

THREE MONTHS AFTER THE HEBREWS HAD left Egypt, they came to the desert of Sinai, pitched their tents, and camped there at the foot of the mount, while Moses went to pray. Moses came back and cautioned the people to sanctify themselves and be prepared for the third day. The people washed themselves and their clothes, and Moses blessed them. And on the third day Moses brought them out of the camp to the foot of the mount. There was great thunder and lightning, and Mt. Sinai quaked and was shrouded in smoke, for the Lord descended upon it in fire. At the sound of loud trumpets God called Moses up to the mount and spoke these words to him:

I am the Lord thy God. Thou shalt have no other Gods before Me.

Thou shalt not take the name of the Lord thy God in vain.

Remember the Sabbath day, to keep it holy. Six days thou shalt labor but on the seventh thou shalt do no work.

Honor thy father and thy mother.

Thou shalt not kill.

Thou shalt be faithful to thy wife.

Thou shalt not steal.

Thou shalt not bear false witness against thy neighbor.

Thou shalt not covet thy neighbor's goods.

Moses told the people all the Lord had said, and they answered, with one voice, "We shall do what the Lord has commanded."

Then the Lord said to Moses, "Come up to Me on the mount and I will give you tablets of stone, with laws and the commandments written so that you may teach the people." Moses went up on the mountain and was hidden by the clouds.

When nearly forty days had passed and Moses had not returned, the people grew anxious and then weary of waiting. And they demanded of Aaron that he create a god to lead them on, for they did not know what had become of Moses. Aaron had the people bring him their golden earrings and jewels, which he melted and made into the shape of a calf. The next morning the people rose early, offered sacrifices before the golden calf, and sat down to feast.

When God saw what they were doing, He became wrathful and sent Moses down with the tablets bearing the commandments. As Moses neared the camp, he heard the noise of the feast, and when he saw the golden calf he became so angry that he threw down the tablets and they were broken. Moses took the calf which they had made, burned it, and ground it to powder. And as a punishment, many of the people were killed.

Moses returned to God and begged Him to forgive the Hebrews. God answered that Moses should return to his people and lead them on toward the Promised Land. He said he would send an angel to lead them, but that one day they would still be punished for having made the golden calf. And He ordered Moses to make two stone tablets like the first and to bring them to Him on the mountain. Moses remained again on the mountain for forty days and forty nights, and wrote down the commandments. And then God commanded the Hebrews to build an ark, in which to house the tablets.

To make the ark (which was concealed in a tent, or tabernacle) the people used precious wood and built a beautiful box, which they covered with gold, inside and out. Gold rings were set in the four corners, and wooden sticks, covered with gold, were slipped through them to carry the ark. They put away the tablets in the ark and carried it with them through all their wanderings.

Balaam's Ass

AS THE ISRAELITES PASSED THROUGH THE lands of different tribes, they found that some were peaceful but others were fearful and warlike and would not let them pass.

To pass through the land of the Amorites, the children of Israel had had to wage war against them. They conquered the Amorites and dwelt for a time in their cities and villages. As they continued on their journey to the Promised Land of Canaan, they came to the plains of Moab, across the Jordan from Jericho. The king of the Moabites, Balak, having heard of the successes of the Israelites against the Amorites, was afraid. Therefore he sent messengers to the false prophet Balaam, saying, "Behold, there is a people come from Egypt. They are covering the face of the earth and are now at my very boundaries. Come now and curse them for me, so that we may battle with them and drive them from the land."

But God said to Balaam, "You shall not go, for these children of Israel are blessed."

Then Balak sent princes from his court as messengers, promising Balaam great honors if he would go. Again Balaam refused—for he would not go against the word of the Lord. But this time God appeared to Balaam saying, "Go with these men, but be sure to do as *I* tell you."

In the morning Balaam saddled his ass and went with the princes of Moab. And God sent an angel who stood before the ass, sword in hand. The ass saw the angel and turned into the field by the road. Balaam struck the ass in order to turn her back into the road.

A little farther on, where the road passed a vineyard with a wall on either side, the angel stood in the way again. The ass thrust herself against the wall, crushing Balaam's foot, so that he beat her again. Then the angel stood in a narrow place where there was no way to turn either to right or left, and the ass fell down under Balaam.

Balaam was so incensed that he beat the ass with his staff. Then the Lord opened the mouth of the ass, and she said, "What have I done that you should beat me so?"

Balaam answered, "Because you have mocked me. If I had a sword I would kill you."

Again the ass spoke, "I have been a faithful ass for many years. Have I ever acted so before?"

Even as Balaam answered "No," the Lord opened his eyes and he saw the angel, and bowed to the ground, realizing that the faithful ass had saved his life. The angel then told Balaam that he might go on, but that he should speak only the words which the Lord put in his mouth.

So when Balaam arrived before the King of Moab, he could only bless the children of Israel, saying, "Blessed is he who blesses you—and cursed is he who curses you!" Then Balak, in great anger, refused to honor Balaam, and sent him back to his own country.

The Death of Moses

AFTER FORTY YEARS OF WANDERING IN THE wilderness, the Hebrews reached the plains of Moab. Moses was growing old and knew that he would not be with his people when they finally reached the Promised Land of Canaan. For a long time he had been writing down all the laws God had given him, and now his work was done.

Moses called Joshua, and before all the Hebrews said to him, "Be strong and have courage. You must lead these people to the land of their fathers. The Lord will be with you. He will not forsake you, so do not fear." And he gave Joshua the book of laws to put in the ark with the stone tablets.

Then Moses went up on the mountain of Nebo—across the Jordan from Jericho—and from there the Lord showed him the plain of the valley of Jericho, the city of palm trees, and all the land that spread between the valley and the River Jordan which they would have to cross. And the Lord said to him, "Behold the land of Canaan. I swore to Abraham, to Isaac, and to Jacob that I would give that land to their children. You have seen it with your eyes, but you shall not cross over into it." Moses called the children of Israel to him and gave them his blessing.

Shortly thereafter Moses died, and was buried in the land of Moab. The children of Israel mourned for thirty days, for he had been a very great prophet, and had led the Hebrews out of their slavery in Egypt.

Joshua was a good leader, full of the spirit of wisdom, but there never again rose a prophet in Israel like Moses, whom the Lord knew face to face.

Joshua

THE MOURNING OVER THE DEATH OF Moses being at an end, Joshua commanded the people to gather their belongings together, to prepare food, and to make ready for the crossing of the Jordan.

He sent two men ahead to spy on the city of Jericho. They entered the city secretly and were given shelter by a woman named Rahab, whose house was built into the city wall. The king of Jericho heard of the spies and ordered Rahab to give them up. But she hid them on her roof, saying they had left when it was dark—about the time of the shutting of the city gate.

She told the two spies that the people of Jericho had heard how the Lord had dried up the Red Sea for the Hebrews as they left Egypt and that they had no courage or wish to fight against such a favored people. She made a bargain to help the two men escape if they would spare her family when Joshua's army conquered the city. Then she took a scarlet rope and let them down through a window, over the wall to the plain outside the city. She bound the scarlet rope around the same window, to mark her house so that it would not be destroyed.

The spies returned and told Joshua what had happened and how the people of Jericho felt. The Hebrews set out immediately on this final stretch of their wanderings. And Joshua led them just as the Lord had commanded him.

When they came to the banks of the Jordan, he chose twelve priests, one from each tribe, who carried the golden ark, and these went ahead of the others. As soon as their feet touched the river, the waters rolled back, leaving a dry path, so that the people could cross the riverbed dryshod into the land of Canaan.

After the crossing, each of the twelve priests picked up a large stone from the riverbed, and placed it as a memorial to mark the spot where the Hebrews had first set foot in Canaan. Immediately the waters of the Jordan flowed again. God commanded this so that in days to come, when children should ask their fathers the meaning of the stones, they could answer that there God had held back the waters for the children of Israel to cross the Jordan. Then all the people of the earth would know how mighty was the Lord and how careful of His children.

The Battle of Jericho

WHEN THE PEOPLE OF JERICHO WIT-nessed the crossing of the Jordan, they were frightened and closed the gates of the city so that no one could go in or out.

As they saw the Hebrews coming, they prepared to fight. But the Hebrews came in a procession led by seven priests carrying trumpets made from rams' horns. They were followed by seven more priests bearing the golden ark, and then by all the soldiers and the people. Once each day for six days they paraded about the city in silence, as the Lord had commanded, led by the priests blowing on their trumpets. On the seventh day, they arose at dawn, and paraded about the city seven times. And after the seventh time, when the priests had blown upon their trumpets, Joshua cried to the people, "Shout! for the Lord has given you the city."

So the Hebrews shouted as the trumpets blew, and the walls of Jericho came tumbling down. The people went into the city and took it, and destroyed all that was in the city—except the house that was marked with the scarlet rope. For Joshua saved Rahab and all her household because she had hidden the messengers he sent to spy on Jericho.

Before Joshua died, he warned the Hebrews to remember how God had always been with them and had led them out of slavery into the rich land of Canaan. The people promised, but after Joshua's death they forgot the Lord and turned to the gods of the tribes that lived about them. God was angry with them, and when neighboring tribes made war on the Hebrews He no longer came to help them. So although they had reached the Promised Land, it was a long time before they could enjoy it in peace.

Gideon

WITHIN A FEW GENERATIONS AFTER THE death of Joshua, the children of Israel had deserted the Lord and had turned to the worship of idols, such as the golden calf Aaron had once made. Therefore, when they were attacked by the Midianites, a tribe to the south, the Lord did not help them.

The Midianites stole their oxen and sheep, destroyed many of the crops, and finally came with their cattle and pitched their tents on the choicest grazing grounds. Many of the Israelites fled to the hills and barely existed in dens and caves, which they turned into strongholds.

In their extremity the children of Israel cried to the Lord to save them. God then sent a prophet to chastise them for having disobeyed Him, but He sent also an angel to choose a leader who would deliver them from the Midianites.

The angel appeared before Gideon, son of Joash in Manasseh, who was threshing some wheat he had hidden from the Midianites. Gideon could not understand why he should be chosen leader of the Hebrews, for, as he said to the angel, "My family is poor and I am the least in my father's house."

God told Gideon that he must destroy the altar of Baal which his father had built, cut down the trees about it, and build an altar to God in its place. Gideon feared his father and the men of the city, so he waited until night to carry out the Lord's command. When he had finished, he offered up a bullock as a sacrifice to God.

When the men of the city came to the altar in the morning and saw what had happened, they went to Joash and said to him, "Bring out your son, that he may die, for he has cast down the altar of Baal and has cut down the grove that was beside it."

But Joash refused, saying, "Why do you plead for Baal? If he is truly a god, let him plead and punish for himself." So the men went away.

Then Gideon sent out messengers to gather the Israelites from near and far to unite in a band and drive away the Midianites.

To be sure that he had really been chosen leader, Gideon asked the Lord for a sign. "Behold!" he said, "I will put a fleece of wool on the ground. If dew falls only on the fleece, and the earth around it be dry, then shall I know that You will save Israel by my hand."

In the morning he rose early and, seeing the earth dry, he picked up the fleece and was able to wring from it a bowlful of dew.

Then Gideon prayed again, "Oh, Lord, do not be angry with me, but give me one more sign. Let it now be dry only on the fleece, and let the dew fall on the ground about it." And God did so that night, for in the morning it was dry on the fleece only, and there was dew on all the ground.

A great many men gathered, anxious to follow a leader who could restore their country to them. But the Lord told Gideon there were too many. Even after Gideon had sent back the men who were afraid, the Lord said there were still so many they would feel that their own strength of numbers had saved them from the Midianites. So Gideon led the men down to the water to drink. Some of them knelt to drink, some lay down and lapped the water like dogs, and others drank from their cupped hands. Of these last there were three hundred, and the Lord said to Gideon, "By these three hundred will I save you."

That night Gideon divided the three hundred men into three companies. To each man he gave a trumpet and an empty pitcher that had a torch in it. Then he told them that when they reached the camp of the Midianites he would blow his trumpet as a signal for the attack.

So Gideon and his soldiers crept silently down upon the enemy camp and surrounded it. When Gideon blew his trumpet, his three hundred followers blew their trumpets also, broke the pitchers, and held aloft the burning torches that had been concealed in them. And they cried out, "The sword of the Lord and of Gideon!"

The Midianites, awakened by the crashing of the pitchers, were terrified to see themselves surrounded, and they fled in all directions. The Israelites pursued them across the Jordan, killing many of the leaders. Thus, with the help of the Lord, did they free themselves once more from the hands of the enemy.

Samson

BUT THE HEBREWS DID NOT FOR LONG hold their land in peace. Many neighboring tribes made war upon them, and, after Gideon, no leader came forward who could bring victory to the Israelites.

The Philistines were a warlike tribe who continually harassed their settlements, and the Hebrews cried out for a leader to conquer these enemies.

In Zorah, in the land of Canaan, there was a man named Manoah who had no children. One day an angel of the Lord appeared to his wife and told her she would have a son who one day would deliver the Hebrews from the Philistines. When their son was born, they named him Samson, and as the angel had instructed them, they did not cut his hair at all; nor, as he grew older, did he shave.

When Samson was a young man he visited the town of Timnath in Philistia, and there he met a young Philistine woman with whom he fell in love. When he came home he told his parents he wanted to marry her. They were very worried, not knowing that this was according to the Lord's plan to give Samson an occasion to quarrel with the Philistines.

According to custom, Samson's parents went with him to Timnath to see the girl. As they approached the town, a young lion came roaring at them. But the Lord suddenly gave Samson enormous strength. The youth seized the lion and tore it to pieces with his bare hands.

Some time later, when he was again traveling to Timnath, Samson passed the place where he had killed the lion. He noticed that a swarm of bees had made a nest in the carcass, and, finding honey, he took some and ate it. He took some to his father and mother, without telling them whence it came.

When Samson was married there was a great feast in Timnath, and among the guests were thirty young Philistine men. To them Samson said, "I will give you a riddle. If you can solve it, give me the answer within a week, and I will give you thirty suits of clothing. If you cannot, then you shall give me thirty suits of clothing." And he gave them this riddle: Out of the eater came forth meat, and out of the strong came forth sweetness. And no one could solve the riddle.

So the Philistine men went to Samson's wife and threatened to burn down her father's house if she did not find out the answer from her husband. At first Samson did not want to tell her, saying as an excuse, "I have not even told my parents. I have told no one. It is a secret." But she wept and pleaded so that finally he told her how he had killed the lion and then found the honey.

She went straight to the Philistines with the answer, and on the seventh day, at the end of the wedding feast, they spoke to Samson. "What is sweeter than honey, and what is stronger than a lion?"

Samson knew that only his wife could have given away the secret, and he was very angry. He left her, went out and slew thirty Philistines, took their clothes, and gave them to the thirty who had solved the riddle. And then he went home to his father's house.

When his anger had passed he returned to Timnath for his wife, but found that her father, thinking Samson no longer loved her, had given her as a wife to another man. For revenge, Samson caught three hundred foxes and, tying firebrands to their tails, sent them running through the Philistines' cornfields, vineyards, and olive groves, so that the crops were all burned. Then he left the town and hid himself in a cave high on a near-by hill, while the

Philistines searched all over for him without success.

After that the Philistines persecuted the Hebrews even more than before. Finally some of the Hebrews, who knew where Samson was hidden, went to him and told him they were going to turn him over to the Philistines so that they might have peace. He agreed to let them bind his hands and arms and to go with them, if they would promise not to harm him.

When they had given him over to the Philistines and were gone, the strength of the Lord came again to Samson, and he broke all the cords with which he had been bound. Seeing the jawbone of a dead ass on the ground, he seized it in his hand as a club and killed a thousand of the Philistines. This exertion made him feel very thirsty and faint, but God caused water to spring out of the jawbone so that Samson could drink and refresh himself. Immediately he regained his strength, and escaped.

The Hebrews were now so impressed by Samson's strength and resourcefulness that they made him their leader.

Samson and Delilah

SOME YEARS LATER, SAMSON FELL IN LOVE with a woman of Sorek who was named Delilah. When the leaders of the Philistines heard of it, they sought to capture Samson with her help. They went to Delilah and promised her great wealth if she could find out the secret of Samson's strength.

The first time that Delilah asked Samson his secret, he was cautious and did not give her a true answer. He told her, "If I am bound with seven green willow branches which have never been dried, then I shall be as weak as other men."

That night as he slept, Delilah bound him with seven green willow branches which the Philistines had brought. Then they hid in the room to see what would happen. In the middle of the night Delilah woke Samson, crying that the Philistines were about to capture him. And Samson arose and broke the branches as easily as if they had been air. The Philistines dared not show themselves, for they saw that Samson was as strong as ever.

Three more times Delilah tried to learn the secret of Samson's strength, but each time Samson told her another story. Once he said that he could not break new ropes which had never been used. Another time he said he would lose his strength if she wove his hair and pinned it up. Each time, the plans of the Philistines failed and they were not able to capture him. Delilah kept after him every day, urging him to tell her. Finally, wearied by her endless questions, Samson told her of the Lord's command that his hair should never be cut—that if it were to be cut he would no longer have his strength.

This time Delilah knew that Samson had really told her his secret. She sent for the Philistine leaders, who came bringing her the eleven hundred pieces of silver they had promised. That night as Samson slept she cut off his long locks of hair, and his great strength left him. Then Delilah woke him, crying, "Samson, the Philistines are here." Samson was now weak, and the Philistines were easily able to take him. They put out his eyes and brought him to Gaza, where they bound him with brass chains and set him to grinding grain in the prison house.

Knowing that he was now blind and that he was securely bound, the Philistines forgot the secret of Samson's strength. Each day, as his hair grew, his strength returned.

One day the lords of the Philistines gathered in the temple to offer sacrifices to their gods and to rejoice at having captured Samson, the only Hebrew who could defeat them. After the ceremonies they spread a great feast and made merry, and they had Samson brought from the prison so that they could make sport of him. When Samson could endure it no longer, he said to the boy who guided him, "Lead me to the pillars that hold up the temple so that I may rest against them."

Then he put an arm around each great pillar and he called to God, "Oh, Lord God, remember me and give me strength that I may have revenge on these Philistines for blinding me." He pulled with all his might and broke the pillars, so that the roof of the temple came down and killed all who were within.

Then Samson's relatives came and took him and buried him in the burying place of his family.

Ruth

IT CAME TO PASS, IN THE DAYS WHEN THE judges ruled, that there was a famine in the land of Canaan. Then Elimelech, of the tribe of Judah, left his home in Bethlehem, took his wife Naomi and his two sons Mahlon and Chilion, and went to dwell in the land of Moab, where there was no famine.

The two sons married Moab women—one named Orpah and the other Ruth, and they dwelt there about ten years. Then great sorrow came to them, for first Elimelech and then his two sons died and Naomi was left alone with her two daughters-in-law.

Moses struck the rock twice, and water came out. (Page 52)

Samson seized the lion and killed it with his bare hands. (Page 67)

Since the famine was now over in her own country, Naomi decided to return to Bethlehem, where she had relatives. Orpah and Ruth wept and grieved that Naomi was leaving, but Naomi felt it was better for them to remain with their families in their own land, where they might remarry. Orpah returned to her people, but Ruth said, "Ask me not to leave you. Whither you go, I will go; and where you lodge, I will lodge. Your people shall be my people, and your God, my God." When Naomi saw that Ruth would be happier going with her, she no longer urged her to return to her people. So the two set forth and journeyed until they came to Bethlehem.

The women who had known Naomi in the old days came to greet her. When they saw her they said, "Is this Naomi?" for she looked so much older and sadder. And she said, "Call me not Naomi; call me Mara, for the Almighty hath dealt very bitterly with me."

It was the beginning of the barley harvest in Bethlehem. Having no store of food or means of support, Ruth said to Naomi, "Let me go to the fields to gather up barley and ears of corn so that we may eat." And she went and gleaned after the reapers in the fields of Boaz—a wealthy man of the town.

Now Boaz came from Bethlehem to see how the harvest was progressing. He spoke to the reapers, "The Lord be with you," and they answered him, "The Lord bless you."

Then Boaz asked the overseer, "Who is this strange young woman?" The overseer answered, "It is Ruth, who came back from the land of Moab with Naomi. She has been working hard all morning."

Boaz went over to Ruth and addressed her kindly, for he had heard the people speak highly of her for her great loyalty to Naomi.

"Stay and glean in these fields and eat and drink with the others," he said.

As she went back to her work Boaz ordered the young men, "Let her glean among the sheaves and reproach her not. And let fall some extra handfuls on purpose that she may gather plenty."

That evening, when Ruth threshed out what she had gleaned, she had about an ephah (a little more than a bushel) of barley. She took it up and brought it to her mother-in-law in the city. And Naomi, amazed, said to her, "Where have you gleaned today? Blessed be the one who has been so good to you."

When Ruth told her where she had worked, Naomi said, "Blessed be he of the Lord who is kind to the living and to the dead. Boaz is a kinsman of Elimelech's—it is good that you should glean with his maidens and not in any other field."

So Ruth dwelt with her mother-in-law and gleaned in the fields of Boaz during the barley and wheat harvests.

There was one kinsman more closely related to Naomi than Boaz. According to Hebrew custom, the nearest of kin has first right to buy the property of a dead man and to marry his widow.

Now Boaz wished to marry Ruth, so he went up to the city gate with the elders of the city to advertise that he wished to buy the property of Elimelech and to marry Ruth. The nearer kinsman agreed to give up his right. According to the way in Israel, he drew off his shoe before witnesses and gave it to Boaz to seal the bargain.

Knowing that Ruth had found favor in the eyes of Boaz and that she returned his affection, Naomi said one evening: "Anoint yourself, dress in your very best, and this night go where Boaz is sleeping on the threshing floor, and there lie at his feet."

Ruth did as her mother-in-law had commanded. When Boaz awoke, he saw Ruth, and his heart was stirred. "You are blessed, Ruth, for you are virtuous and loyal, and have not sought after the young men."

So Ruth and Boaz were married—and all the people that were about were highly pleased that their neighbor had found such a good wife. And they compared Ruth to Rachel and Leah, who first built up the house of Israel.

Naomi was happy, for as her neighbors said, "Your daughter-in-law loves you and has been better to you than seven sons could be." But she was soon to be happier still, for Ruth bore a fine young son, and Naomi became his nurse.

The boy was named Obed, who when he grew up was the father of Jesse and the grandfather of David.

Samuel

THE PHILISTINES WERE STILL THE BITTER enemies of the Hebrews. They were powerful and had large armies which were continually attacking Hebrew towns.

There was among the Hebrews a man named Samuel, whose mother had dedicated him to God when he was a baby. He had grown up serving the priests in the temple, and as he grew older, God saw that he was very good and He appeared before him and spoke to him. The people all about came to know that God talked to him, so that when Samuel grew up he became a prophet of the Lord and a judge among the Hebrews.

When Samuel was old, he made his sons judges over Israel. But his sons were not like him. They were dishonest, took bribes, and did not judge fairly. So the elders of the tribes of Israel came to Samuel and complained. They insisted that he choose a king to rule over Israel, to go out before them and fight their battles like the rulers of all the other nations. Samuel was very displeased that the Hebrews should reject God as their leader and want a king instead.

He pointed out that their sons would be taken to be the king's horsemen and charioteers, soldiers and workers; their daughters would be taken as cooks and bakers; the king would take the best of their fields, their flocks, and their servants. When all these things had happened, they would regret it and cry out, but in that day it would be too late and the Lord would not hear them. Nevertheless, the people refused to follow this advice and insisted on a king. The Lord told Samuel to do as the people wished, and give them a king. He said that he would send to Samuel a man from the land of Benjamin, and this man would be king over Israel.

Samuel Chooses a King

NOW THERE WAS A MAN OF THE TRIBE OF Benjamin whose name was Kish, and he had a son whose name was Saul. There was not among the children of Israel a more presentable person than Saul. He was handsome and a head taller than any of his fellows.

It chanced that the asses of Kish had strayed, and Saul

took one of his father's servants to seek them. In his search he came to Samuel's town, and went to the temple to ask the prophet where to look for the lost animals.

When Samuel saw Saul, the Lord said to him, "Behold the man of whom I spoke! This same shall reign over my people."

Though Saul protested that the Benjamites were the smallest of the tribes of Israel, and his family the least of all the families of the tribe of Benjamin, Samuel ordered a feast for him and anointed him with oil.

Then Samuel called all the tribes of Israel, brought Saul before them, and said, "See him whom the Lord has chosen. There is none like him among all the people."

As the people beheld Saul, towering head and shoulders above the crowd, some of them shouted: "Long live the king!" Others, however, muttered: "He is but a common fellow from the tribe of Benjamin." But Saul held his peace, and returned to his father's house.

Saul's First Battle

NOW THERE WERE SOME TIMID ISRAELITES who wished to make a cowardly treaty with their enemies, the Ammonites. The latter were willing enough, yet they said: "We will grant you a treaty, but as a sign of surrender, we will bore out the right eye of every Israel-ite." A seven-day truce was granted, and there was great sorrowing throughout the land over the harsh terms.

As Saul drove the herds in from his father's fields, he heard the wailing of the people. When he had learned the cause, his anger kindled, and, filled with the spirit of the Lord, he hewed a yoke of oxen into pieces, and sent mes-sengers throughout Israel, saying: "This shall be done to the oxen of those who will not follow Saul and Samuel!"

Then the Israelites gathered around Saul as their leader against the Ammonites. He divided his people into three companies, and attacking at daybreak, they fought fiercely till noonday. The Ammonites lay dead by the thousands, and so scattered were the survivors that not two were left together.

The victorious hosts of Israel then marched to Gilgal, where they proclaimed Saul their king, and offered sacri-fices to Jehovah. And great was the rejoicing among the Israelites!

The Bravery of Jonathan

WHEN SAUL HAD REIGNED FOR TWO years, great armies of the Philistines gathered to fight against Israel. So numerous were the soldiers, chariots, and horsemen that most of the men of Israel hid themselves in caves and thickets and in high places, leaving Saul with only about six hundred men.

Jonathan, Saul's son, called to his armor-bearer, "Let us go over to the garrison of the Philistines. Perhaps the Lord will help us, for He can save by a few as well as by many."

When they had crept over to the garrison, the Philistines, seeing them, thought all the Hebrews were coming out. As they came forward, Jonathan rose up and, with his armor-bearer, killed about twenty men.

Suddenly there was a great trembling in the field, and the earth quaked, causing the Philistines to flee, pursued by Saul's army and even by those who had hidden themselves in the hills.

The battle and pursuit raged through the day, and the Hebrew soldiers were greatly distressed, for Saul had ordered that the man would be cursed who should eat any food until evening, when they had revenged themselves on their enemies.

As the Hebrews pursued the Philistines, they went through a wood where the honey was dropping from a tree. Though they were faint with hunger, they dared not touch it for fear of Saul's curse.

But Jonathan, who had not heard his father's charge, dipped his staff in a honeycomb, ate, and was refreshed. Then some of the others told Jonathan of his father's order. Jonathan was angered, and retorted, "My father has troubled the land. See how refreshed I am. If all the people had eaten today, how much greater would have been our success against the Philistines!"

Saul wanted to know whether or not he should pursue the Philistines by night, so he built an altar to the Lord and asked His counsel. But he had no answer—and thus he was sure that someone had violated his order and must therefore die. When he found that it was his own son Jonathan, he said, "You shall surely die!"

But the people and soldiers set up a great protest. "God forbid!" they shouted. "Not one hair of his head shall fall to the ground. For this day God has fought at his side and he has saved Israel." So the people rescued Jonathan from the wrath of his father.

For a time Saul was a good and wise king, and he followed the Lord. But when he had won a few victories over the Philistines his head was turned. He became proud and rebelled against the Lord's commands. God told Samuel that he was displeased with Saul as king of the Hebrews. Samuel told this to Saul, then left him, and never saw him again.

There came a day when God said to Samuel, "How long are you going to weep over Saul? Fill your horn with oil and go to Bethlehem, for there, among the sons of Jesse, the grandson of Ruth and Boaz, I have chosen a king."

Samuel did as he was told and found that God had chosen Jesse's youngest son, David, who tended his father's sheep and played the harp with skill. Then Samuel took the horn of oil and anointed David, and the spirit of the Lord was with David from that day on. At the same time the spirit of the Lord left Saul, and he was greatly troubled.

Saul's servants were worried about their king. He had always been excitable, but when he learned that God had rejected him, he began to have spells of gloominess. In order to calm him when he was troubled, his servants begged him to find a man who could play the harp and perhaps soothe him. One of them said, "I have heard the young son of Jesse in Bethlehem, who plays beautifully. He is strong, handsome, and wise, and the Lord is with him."

Messengers were sent to bring David. When Saul saw him and heard him play, he liked David so much that he made the boy his armor-bearer so that he would always be near him. Whenever Saul was deeply troubled, David took his harp and played for him, and Saul was refreshed and the evil spirit departed from him. Saul grew to love David as he loved his own son, Jonathan.

David and Goliath

ONCE MORE THE PHILISTINES GATHERED together their great armies to battle against the Hebrews. They camped on the side of a mountain, and the Hebrews camped on another mountain with the valley of Elah between them.

One morning there came out from the camp of the Philistines a great giant, Goliath of Gath, who was over nine feet tall. He was covered from head to foot with heavy armor. He carried a huge spear and had a shield-bearer before him.

He came down to the valley and, in a thundering voice, cried out to the armies of the Hebrews, "Why do you not come out and fight? Choose a man from your midst and let him come to fight me. If he can kill me, we will be your servants. But if I win and kill him, then you shall serve us."

When Saul and the Hebrews saw this great giant, they were terrified, for they believed that no one of them could beat him.

Every morning and evening, for forty days, Goliath came down and defied the Hebrews.

Now David had gone home to help his old father with the sheep, for his elder brothers were soldiers in Saul's army. One day Jesse sent David with fresh bread and corn for his brothers, and gifts of fine cheeses for their captains.

David left the sheep with a keeper and went as his father told him. When he came to the battleground, he found the armies set for battle, for the Hebrews had not found any-one to fight Goliath. When David heard Goliath utter his challenge, he went to Saul and begged to be allowed to do battle with the giant.

At first Saul would not hear of it, for he was sure David would be killed. Then David told Saul how once a lion and a bear had attacked his father's sheep and had taken a lamb. He had rescued the lamb and killed both the lion and the bear. Since God had helped him then, he felt sure God would help him against Goliath.

So Saul had David covered with heavy armor to protect him, and gave him a fine sword. But these weapons were too heavy, and David did not know how to handle them; so he took them all off. Then, from the brook that ran through the valley, David chose five smooth stones and put them in his shepherd's bag. He carried his staff in one hand and in the other the sling with which he used to drive off the wild animals that attacked his flocks. And he went down to the valley before Goliath.

When the Philistine looked about and saw this young boy, he roared, half in amusement, half in anger, "Am I a dog that you come after me with a staff? Come, I will feed you to the fowls of the air and the beasts of the field."

David answered, "You come with a sword, a spear, and

David took good aim and swung the sling toward Goliath. (Page 86)

David stole forward and cut off part of Saul's garment. (Page 92)

a shield. I come in the name of the Lord of hosts, the God of the armies of Israel, Whom you have defied. This day God will deliver you into my hand. And I will smite you and take your head from you, that all the earth may know there is a God in Israel."

Then David put his hand in his bag, took out a stone, and put it in his sling. He took good aim and swung the sling toward Goliath. The hurtling stone sank into the giant's forehead, and he fell dead.

David then ran up to the prostrate giant, drew out Goliath's sword, and cut off his head.

When the Philistines saw their champion was dead, they fled. But the Hebrews pursued them and defeated them. Then the victors returned and carried off the spoils from the Philistine tents.

David and Jonathan

THAT DAY SAUL TOOK DAVID INTO HIS household and would not let him return to his home. And there Saul's brave son, Jonathan, was much in his company, and his own courageous soul reached out to the youth who had slain Goliath.

Jonathan and David made a covenant, vowing love and friendship throughout their lives. To seal it, as was the custom, Jonathan took off his coat and gave it to David, along with his sword and bow.

And David went about his business and behaved himself wisely. Saul set him over the men-at-arms, and he was accepted as their leader in the sight of all the people and also in the sight of Saul's servants.

As the victorious soldiers returned from pursuit of the Philistines, the people came out of the cities of Israel to meet the king. The women, rejoicing, sang their praises: "Saul hath slain his thousands, and David his tens of thousands."

These words were displeasing to Saul, and jealousy of his young armor-bearer, David, crept into his heart. The thought came to him: "Soon they will want to make him king."

One day when Saul was troubled, David as usual played the harp for him in the king's chamber. There was a javelin in Saul's hand, and suddenly overcome by black rage he hurled it at the crouching youth. But David avoided the thrust. Then Saul was afraid, for he realized that the Lord had departed from him and was with David. So he sent David away from him, and made him captain over a division of the army, hoping he might be killed in battle. But David went unharmed, and acted so wisely that the people grew to love him. This only made Saul more angry and jealous of his captain.

Then, to make him even more unhappy, Saul learned that his younger daughter Michal had fallen in love with David. David, of course, being originally but a poor shepherd boy, had no hope of marrying a princess. But Saul, thinking he had found a way to rid himself of David, had one of his servants tell him, "The king does not want a dowry. But kill a hundred Philistines within a certain period and you shall marry Michal."

David went out with his men and slew two hundred Philistines before the given time had elapsed, and won Michal for his wife. But he won, too, the ever deeper hatred of the jealous king. He even sought to persuade Jonathan to slay his friend. But Jonathan reasoned gently with his father and reminded him of the many proofs of David's service to his king and country.

Saul sent messengers to David's house to waylay him and slay him as he slept. Michal heard of the plan. She helped

David to escape, by putting an image in his bed so that the murderers would be deceived. Then she lowered her husband down the wall from a window, and he escaped.

So David fled to Samuel, in Ramah, and told him all that Saul had done to him. And he remained there with Samuel.

When Saul heard that David was with Samuel in Ramah, he went after David. But David fled and came back to Jonathan, asking, "What wrong have I done your father that he should seek my life?"

Jonathan answered, "God forbid. You shall not die. My father does nothing without first telling me. Why should he hide this from me? It is not so."

But David swore it was so, saying, "Your father knows what good friends we are, and does not tell you of his wish to kill me, lest you grieve. I tell you, there is but a step between me and death."

Then Jonathan, still not quite believing, said, "I will do whatever you want to help you."

So the two friends decided upon a plan which would let David know how the king felt toward him. David was to be away himself from the king's table at the Feast of the New Moon, hiding meanwhile in the fields for three days. If Saul missed him, but made no complaint, then David would return. But if the king became angry, then David would know that Saul sought his life. They arranged a signal so that if this happened Jonathan's friend would be warned. Accordingly, on the next day, which was the festival of the new moon, David stayed away from the king's table and hid himself in a cave in the fields. When the new moon arose, the king sat down to eat, as at other times, upon a seat by the wall. Jonathan and Abner sat by his side, but David's place was empty.

The first day Saul said nothing. But the next day he asked where David was. Jonathan answered that he had gone to a sacrifice for his family in the city and had begged to be excused.

Then Saul's anger arose, even against Jonathan, and he said, "You have chosen this son of Jesse as your friend. As long as he lives, you shall not be my rightful heir to the throne of Israel. Send and fetch him to me, for he shall surely die."

When Jonathan tried to reason with his father, asking, "Why should he be slain? What has he done?" Saul lost his temper and hurled a javelin at his own son.

Jonathan knew then that his father was determined to slay David. He arose from the table in fierce anger and would not eat, for he was ashamed of his father and his heart was filled with anxiety for David.

In the morning Jonathan took his bow and arrows, and went out with a little lad into the field at the time appointed with David.

Jonathan shot three arrows past the cave where David was hiding. When the lad ran to gather them, Jonathan called out, "Make speed—haste—stay not." But David knew that Jonathan was really speaking to him.

As soon as the lad was gone, David came out from his hiding place. He and Jonathan embraced one another and wept bitterly.

Jonathan said to David, "Go in peace, for we have both sworn in the name of the Lord that He shall be with us and with our children forever." Then David departed, an outlaw, and Jonathan returned to the city.

David Spares Saul's Life

SO DAVID BECAME A FUGITIVE FROM THE
wrath of Saul. With a band of loyal followers, he went
to live in the wilderness, and in the rocky caves on the
mountainsides, always in fear that Saul or his men might
find them and attack them. For Saul still feared the power
and popularity of David among the people.

Once when Saul was returning from a battle with the
Philistines, he was told that David was hiding in the rocky
wilderness of Engedi. Saul, eager to catch this man whom
he regarded as his enemy, took three thousand chosen men
and set out to find David and his men in their strongholds.
Entering the wilderness, Saul with his guards slept that
night in the front part of the large cave in which David and
his men were hiding. Saul never suspected that the outlaws
he sought were there.

During the night when Saul and his followers slept,
David stole forward and cut off part of Saul's garment. But
he would not harm him, nor would he allow his men to
touch him, for he was still loyal to his king.

In the morning, Saul and his host left the cave to resume

their search for David. As they left, David went forth after them and called to Saul: "My lord the king!"

David bowed, and then while Saul listened in astonishment, told of his loyalty and of how he had spared Saul's life during the night.

Saul, recognizing David, wept. He said, "You are more righteous than I. You have done good for evil, and the Lord shall surely reward you. I know that you shall surely be king of Israel."

David then promised Saul that whatever happened he would always be a friend of Saul's descendants and respect his name.

Saul now returned home, and David went back with his men to their mountain stronghold.

But Saul, still fearing David, again sent men out to try to kill him. So David said to himself at last, "One day Saul or his men may catch me and kill me. I must go to the land of the Philistines. Then Saul will know he cannot capture or kill me and he will no longer hunt me."

So David, with his family and the six hundred men that were with him, went to live among the Philistines at Gath. And when Saul heard that David had fled, he no longer hunted him.

The Death of Saul

WHILE DAVID WAS STILL AN OUTLAW, Samuel died, and thus Saul was left greatly in need of a prophet to advise him. For the Philistines were continually threatening the Israelites, and Saul knew not whether to attack or flee before them. He prayed for a sign, but no sign came.

So Saul disguised himself, and with two men went by night to a woman of Endor, known as a witch and a soothsayer. He thought she might help him.

"Call up Samuel for me!" cried the king to the witch when he saw her.

The witch called up Samuel, and Saul heard the prophet's voice speaking thus:

"Why have you disturbed me? Jehovah has refused to answer your prayers, because of your wickedness. The authority shall be taken from you and given to David. Tomorrow you and your sons shall be slain, and your army shall be overpowered by the Philistines."

Saul trembled with fear, and his strength failed him, as he returned to his house.

The next day, even as the spirit of Samuel had foretold, the great host of the Philistines attacked the Israelites, and the battle went against Saul. Soon brave Jonathan and his two brothers fell, and an enemy arrow pierced Saul.

"Draw your sword and kill me," Saul begged of his armor-bearer. "Do not let me fall into the hands of the Philistines to be tortured." When his servant refused, Saul took his own sword and fell upon it.

So ended the house of Saul, even as the witch of Endor had prophesied.

David Becomes King

DAVID MOURNED FOR SAUL AND JONAthan, and then, as God commanded him, he went to live in Hebron. And the men of the tribe of Judah made him leader and king. Immediately Abner, the captain of Saul's army, proclaimed Ishabasheth, one of Saul's sons, king of the tribe of Benjamin and all Israel, and there was long war between the house of Saul and the house of David. But David grew stronger and stronger, and the house of Saul grew weaker and weaker.

Finally the leaders of all the twelve tribes of Israel came to David to ask him to become king over Israel. David took the stronghold of Zion in Jerusalem, and it was named the City of David. They built him a great house of cedar and stone and proclaimed him king. David led the armies against the Philistines and the Moabites and the Syrians, and conquered them all. He dedicated the spoils of these nations to God. He reigned over all Israel forty years and gave judgment and justice to all his people.

David never forgot Jonathan. He sent messengers to see if there were by chance anyone left of the house of Saul. There was a servant, Ziba, who when he was brought before David, said, "There lives, hidden, a son of Jonathan, who is lame in both feet."

Then King David sent for Jonathan's son. When Mephibosheth came into David's presence, he fell on his face before him.

And David said to him, "Fear not; for I will surely show you kindness for Jonathan your father's sake."

Then David gave to Mephibosheth all that had belonged to Saul and Jonathan. And he ordered Ziba and his servants to serve him and till the land for him. And Mephibosheth dwelt in Jerusalem and ate at the king's table, as one of the king's sons.

David and Bathsheba

ONE EVENING, AS DAVID WAS TAKING A walk on the roof of his palace, he saw bathing in a neighboring house a beautiful woman. He inquired after her and found she was Bathsheba, wife of Uriah, the Hittite. David fell in love with her and wished to marry her—so he devised a wicked plan whereby he might do so.

He sent word to Joab, the captain of his armies, to put Uriah in the forefront of the hottest battle and leave him there, so that he might be killed. That very day Uriah was among the valiant slain in battle.

When Uriah's wife heard the news, she mourned for him. When the mourning was past, David sent and fetched her to his house, and she became his wife and bore him a son.

But the Lord was displeased with what David had done and sent Nathan, the prophet, to him.

"There were two men in one city: one rich, the other

poor," said Nathan. "The rich man had many flocks and herds; the poor man had but one ewe lamb, which was the pet of his children. One day, to prepare a meal for a traveler, the rich man passed over his own flocks but took the poor man's lamb and had it prepared for his dinner."

David's anger was kindled against the rich man and he said, "The man who has done this thing shall surely die."

"You are that man," answered Nathan. "Though God delivered you from the hand of Saul, gave you his house and wives, you had Uriah killed so that you could take his wife from him."

David had nothing to say, for he knew that what he had done was wicked. Nathan said, "You shall not die. But because by this deed you gave occasion to the enemies of the Lord to blaspheme, the child that was born shall die."

And the child which Bathsheba bore him sickened and died. While he was sick, David fasted and prayed, hoping the Lord might spare him, but when the baby was dead David knew he had been punished. He ceased his fasting and went to comfort his wife.

Within the year, Bathsheba bore him another son, whom they called Solomon; and the Lord loved Solomon.

The Unfaithful Absalom

AMONG DAVID'S SONS, HIS FAVORITE WAS AB-
salom, a fine, handsome youth. He had many chariots and horses, and when he went driving he had fifty men
to run before him.

As David grew old, Absalom made up his mind that he
rather than Solomon should succeed his father as king. He
even sought to displace his father on the throne. So he set
out to win the hearts of the people. Early in the morning
he rose and went to the city gates. When he saw people
coming in to the king for a judgment, he told them that the
king had sent no one to hear their cases—and then he spoke
of how fair he would be if only he were judge over the land.

Then Absalom left Jerusalem and went to Hebron,
where he gathered about him the followers he had won.
Only then did David hear of Absalom's conspiracy to take
the throne.

David left Jerusalem with his household and many of
his people. He did not want to fight Absalom, neither did
he want the city demolished in battle. Then Absalom returned in triumph to set himself up as king in Jerusalem.

But David's counselors and followers finally prevailed
upon him to take up arms against Absalom and regain his
throne. That night they all passed over the Jordan, and
people of the country brought beds and basins so that

David and his followers might wash, drink, and rest. They also brought flour, barley, beans and honey, butter, cheese, and meat, so that they might eat and refresh themselves.

Then David divided his followers into three companies, but when he went forth to lead them they all protested. "Remain here," they pleaded. "If we flee or are defeated it does not matter. But you are worth ten thousand of us. Stay, that you may help us later in the city."

David agreed to do as they thought best, and remained by the city gate. But he commanded Joab and the other captains to deal gently with Absalom when they should come upon him.

So the people went out to battle in the wood of Ephraim, and they defeated the renegades. Absalom fled on his mule, but as the mule passed under a great oak in the forest, Absalom was caught in its branches while the mule went on. Then Joab came up and thrust three darts through Absalom's heart.

When the news of Absalom's death reached David, he wept, "O Absalom, my son! Would to God I had died for you! My son! My son!"

The victory was turned to mourning, for the people saw how the king grieved for his son, and they stole back into the city as if ashamed.

Then Joab came before David and said, "You shame the people who followed you faithfully and who this day did save your life and the lives of all your household. It would seem that if Absalom had lived and we all had died in battle, you would be well pleased. Forget your own personal grief in the joy of your loyal people."

So the king arose and went forth and spoke to the people, and they returned in triumph to Jerusalem.

King Solomon

WHEN DAVID WAS OLD AND WEAK AND could no longer attend to the affairs of his kingdom himself, he named his son Solomon to be king in his stead.

Solomon loved the Lord and followed His commands and made many offerings to Him. One day Solomon went up to Gibeon, a high mountain, to offer sacrifices. That night God appeared to Solomon in a dream and said, "What shall I give you?"

Solomon answered, "O Lord, You showed great mercy to David my father, and now You have made me king in his stead over a great people. Give me, therefore, an understanding heart so that I may surely know good from evil and judge Thy people well."

The Lord was well pleased with Solomon's answer, and said, "Because you did not ask for great riches or a long life, because you did not ask that I kill your enemies, I have done as you asked. I have given you a wise and understanding heart, like no one before you and no one that shall follow you. I have also given you what you did not ask for, both riches and honor, so that there shall not be another king like you. If you walk in My ways and keep My commandments, then I will give you a long life."

And Solomon grew rich and powerful, and reigned for many years with justice and mercy. Three thousand proverbs did he write, and many beautiful songs. And he became, as God had promised, the wisest king of all time.

The Wisdom of Solomon

ONE DAY TWO WOMEN CAME BEFORE KING Solomon to ask him to settle their dispute.

One woman said, "This woman and I dwell in one house. I gave birth to a child, and three days later so did she. There was no stranger with us in the house.

"In the night this woman's child died. At midnight she arose, took my son from beside me while I slept, and laid her dead child by me.

"When I rose in the morning I found the dead child. But when I looked at it, it was not my son."

Then the other woman interrupted to say, "No, the living child is my son, and the dead one hers." And they quarreled until Solomon said, "Bring me a sword!"

When the sword was handed him, he said, "Divide the living child in two. Give half to the one and half to the other."

Then the first woman, who was the real mother, cried out, "O my lord, give her the living child, but do not slay it."

But the second woman said, "Let it be neither mine nor yours. Let it be divided."

Then the king answered, "Do not divide it. Give the living child to the first woman, for she is the true mother."

And all Israel heard of the judgment and feared the king, for they saw that the wisdom of God was in him.

Building the Temple

IT WAS IN THE FOURTH YEAR OF KING SOLOmon's rule that he began what was to be remembered as his greatest accomplishment, the building of the temple at Jerusalem. The site selected was Mount Moriah, where in years past the Lord had appeared to David on the threshing floor.

It was ninety feet long, thirty feet wide, and three stories in height, with ample wings and a noble porch. Hundreds of artisans had labored in the forests and quarries hewing the timbers and dressing the stone, for the outside was built entirely of stone, while the interior was completely lined with cedar of Lebanon. Winding stairways led to the floors above, and an inner room was prepared to hold the ark, guarded by two huge winged bulls carved from olive wood. And much gold and brass and many precious stones were used in making Solomon's temple the most beautiful yet built by the hand of man.

The building was many years in construction, but at last came the day of its completion. Then Solomon commanded the priests to bear the ark with its two tablets of stone which Moses had placed within it, so many years ago, and the sacred tent and the sacred vessels, and to place them all within the inner room of the temple.

And as they did so, a cloud filled the entire temple, and Solomon stood before the brazen altar, and in the presence of a great assembly of his people, gave thanks to Jehovah for having kept the promise He had made to David.

King Solomon and the Queen of Sheba

S O GREAT WAS THE FAME OF KING SOLOMON that it reached into the kingdoms of the south, and word of it was brought even to the Queen of Sheba by travelers and merchants from distant lands. Doubtless the stories of the Hebrew king's wisdom and judgment, of his navies which brought him treasures from all the world, of his beautiful palaces, his thrones of solid gold, his armies of horsemen and charioteers, grew with the telling.

There came a day when the beautiful Queen decided that she would go to Jerusalem to see for herself whether the tales were true. Bringing rich gifts and a train of servants, she presented herself before Solomon's throne to ask him many difficult questions, all of which the king answered from the great depth and breadth of his wisdom.

The Queen listened, and when he had answered her final question, she said: "I did not believe the tales that were told, O Solomon, but I see now that they were true, and more, for your wisdom and your riches are truly great. Surely God has delighted in you to make you such a noble and wise ruler."

And after bestowing upon him many rare gifts from her treasury, Sheba returned to her own country to ponder the things she had learned from Solomon.

The Kingdom Divided

IN HIS OLD AGE KING SOLOMON TURNED away from God and worshiped other gods. And because of his tyranny the land of Israel became torn by dissension and rebellion. The arch-plotter against the rule of the aged monarch was Solomon's chief governor, Jeroboam.

One day the latter met the prophet Ahijah in a field outside Jerusalem. Seizing the new garment with which he was clad, the prophet rent it into twelve pieces. "Because of Solomon's sins, thus shall Jehovah rend Israel out of the hands of Solomon," he cried. "Only one tribe for David's sake shall remain under the rule of Solomon's son, while you shall be made king over the rest of the tribes."

After Solomon's death, his son Rehoboam ascended the throne. Jeroboam asked of the new ruler whether he would lighten the people's burdens. But the headstrong Rehoboam, scorning the advice of the old men of his council, replied: "My father chastised you with whips, but I shall chastise you with scorpions!"

When the Israelites received this answer, they no longer hesitated. All but the tribe of Judah rebelled against Rehoboam and the House of David, and they stoned his tax-gatherers to death. Rehoboam fled in his chariot to Jerusalem, and Jeroboam ruled over the rest of Israel.

And so troublous times once more came to the children of Israel.

Elijah and the Widow Woman

ABOUT SIXTY YEARS AFTER THE DIVISION OF Israel into two kingdoms, Asa, a good king who did what was right in the eyes of the Lord, ruled in Judah, while Ahab ruled in Samaria.

It came to pass that Ahab, who did evil in the sight of the Lord, took as a wife Jezebel, a princess of Zidonia who worshiped Baal. Ahab planted a grove and reared up an altar and a temple to Baal in Samaria. Ahab did more to provoke the Lord God of Israel to anger than all the kings of Israel who had preceded him.

Then did the prophet Elijah the Tishbite say unto Ahab, "According to the word of the Lord God of Israel, there shall be neither rain nor dew in the land for many years."

Lest the people blame Elijah for the drought he had prophesied, God sent him to hide himself by a brook, Cherith, near Jordan, and He commanded the ravens to feed him. After a while, since there was no rain, the brook dried up. Then God sent Elijah to dwell in Zarephath, saying, "I have commanded a widow woman there to feed you."

Elijah did as he was told, and when he came to the gates of the city, he met the widow gathering sticks. He called to her and said, "Bring me a little water, for I am very thirsty, and a morsel of bread."

The widow answered, "A little water I can bring you, but I have no bread, only a handful of meal in a barrel and a little oil left in my pitcher. I am gathering sticks now to cook it for me and my son so that we may eat before we die."

And Elijah said to her, "Do as you have said, but also give some to me. For the Lord has said that neither the barrel nor the pitcher shall be empty until the day He sends rain to end the famine." And they had food for many days from the widow's small store.

Then the widow's son fell sick and was near death. The poor woman went to Elijah and cried, "What have I done that my son should die?"

Elijah carried the boy down to his mother. (Page 109)

Elijah ran before Ahab's chariot to the gates of the city. (Page 111)

Elijah took her son and carried him up into the loft where he slept, and laid him on his own bed.

He cried to God, "O Lord, why do You bring evil upon the widow who has fed me?" And he bowed beside the child and prayed, "O Lord, my God, let this child live."

The Lord heard the voice of Elijah, and the child revived. Elijah took the boy, carried him down to his mother, and said, "See, your son lives."

Then the widow answered, "Now I know that you are a true prophet of God and that you speak the words of the Lord."

In the third year of the drought, the Lord came to Elijah and said, "Go before Ahab in Samaria, and I will send rain upon the earth."

When Ahab saw Elijah he said, "Is it you who have brought this drought and famine to Israel?"

Fearlessly Elijah made answer, "It is you, your wife Jezebel, and your household who have forsaken the commandments of the Lord. You are responsible for Israel's trouble. You have ordered the destruction of the prophets of the Lord, but the prophets of Baal flourish. Therefore send for them to gather on Mt. Carmel all the prophets of Baal, and the people of Israel."

When they were all gathered together, Elijah spoke to them. "How long will it take you to make up your minds? If the Lord is God, follow Him; if not, then follow Baal."

The people, completely awed by seeing Elijah so fearless, answered not a word.

"I alone am prophet of the Lord," he went on, "but there are here four hundred and fifty prophets of Baal. Give us therefore two bullocks to sacrifice. Let them choose one, kill and prepare it, lay it on wood but put no fire under it. I will do likewise. Then let them call on Baal to light their fire, and I will call on the Lord. Let the one who answers be your God."

The people were willing, so the sacrifices were prepared. The prophets of Baal prayed all morning. They cried aloud, and tore their garments, but there was no answer of any kind—their sacrifice did not burn.

When evening fell, Elijah came forward. He took twelve stones, representing the twelve tribes of Israel, and made an altar. He dug a trench round about the altar; he cut the bull into pieces and laid it on the wood which he had set in order. Then he said to the people, "Fill four barrels with water and pour it over the sacrifice and on the wood." They did so three times, until the trench was filled with water.

Then Elijah prayed aloud, "O Lord, God of Abraham, Isaac, and of Israel! Let it be known that You are God of Israel, that I am Your servant and have done only as You have commanded. Hear me, so that these people may know You are the true God and will turn their hearts to You again."

And the fire of the Lord fell and consumed not only the sacrifice, the wood, and the stones but all the water in the trench as well.

When the people saw it they fell to the ground on their faces, saying, "The Lord is our God." And Elijah said to them, "Take the prophets of Baal; let not one of them escape." And they took them and slew them, every one.

Elijah now said to Ahab, "Get up. Eat and drink, for there will be an abundance of rain."

A strong wind blew up, driving great black rain clouds across the sky. Ahab got into his chariot to ride down to the city before the great rain should overtake him. As the storm broke, the hand of the Lord gave strength to Elijah, and he ran the whole way before Ahab to the entrance of the city.

When Ahab told Jezebel all that Elijah had done, and how he had slain all the prophets of Baal, Jezebel was furious. She sent this message to Elijah: "Let the gods do the same to me if I do not take your life, as you took the lives of the prophets, by this time tomorrow."

Therefore Elijah once more fled from the city. During his flight the Lord pointed out to him one named Elisha, whom he should anoint to follow him as prophet. On his way back to Damascus, Elijah passed a man plowing behind some oxen in the field. It was Elisha, whom God had chosen to be prophet in his place. The older man threw his mantle over the plowman, and Elisha, pausing only to kiss his father and mother farewell, followed after Elijah and served him.

Long after, when Elijah was old and the Lord was ready to take him into heaven, he led Elisha down to the Jordan. While fifty of the sons of the prophets stood to watch from afar, Elijah took off his mantle, smote the waters so that they were divided, and the two crossed on dry ground to the other side.

Then Elijah said, "Ask what I shall do for you before I am taken away."

And Elisha answered, "I pray that a double portion of your spirit be within me."

"You have asked a very difficult thing," Elijah told him.

"Nevertheless, if you see me when I am taken from you it shall be so. If not, your prayer will not be answered."

As they still talked, there appeared a chariot of fire and horses of fire that swept between them and bore Elijah into heaven in a whirlwind.

And Elisha saw it and cried out, "My father! My father! The chariot and horsemen of Israel!"

He picked up the mantle which had fallen from Elijah and smote the waters of the Jordan. When they parted so that he could recross on dry ground, the sons of the prophets came and bowed before him. For they saw that the spirit of Elijah rested on Elisha.

Elisha

AND SO ELISHA CONTINUED THE WORK OF Elijah. Many were the miracles he performed as he traveled through the land of Israel.

There was a Shunammite woman (Shunem was on the north side of the Vale of Jezreel) who had only one son, whom she dearly loved. Each day he went into the fields with his father to help the reapers. One day the lad fell sick, and after they had carried him home to his mother, he died.

The mother laid him upon a bed, and set forth to seek

Elisha, the man of God, who had helped her in times past. Seeing that she was greatly troubled, the prophet went with her to her house where the child lay. And he went into the room alone, and shut the door and prayed. Suddenly the boy sneezed seven times, and sat up, and opened his eyes.

And the man of God said: "Call the Shunammite." And when she had come, he said: "Take up your son."

Falling at his feet, the mother poured out her thanks to Elisha for saving her son.

Upon another occasion Elisha and his followers chanced to be in the land of Gilgal during a time of great famine.

Calling to his servants, he said: "Let the great pot be put on the fire, and cook pottage."

All that could be found in the fields was a wild vine bearing gourds, and these were shredded into the pot. Then all ate of the pottage and found it good.

Later there came a man from Baalshalisha, bringing with him bread and twenty barley loaves and some ears of corn in the husk. Elisha directed his servants to distribute this food to all of the people roundabout, but they cried: "My master, that little is not enough to set before so many."

Elisha answered: "God has promised that they shall eat and leave thereof. Set the food before the people."

So the servants did as he bade them, and all the people

ate their fill, and there was food left over when they had finished, even as the man of God had said.

Naaman, the Leper

NAAMAN, THE CAPTAIN OF THE ARMIES OF the king of Syria, was a great man, but he was afflicted with a terrible illness. He was a leper.

The Syrians had made war on the Hebrews and, at different times, had taken some of them captive. Among these was a little girl from Samaria who waited on Naaman's wife.

One day she said to her mistress, "If only Naaman would go to the prophet in Samaria, he would be cured of his leprosy!"

The woman repeated the story to her husband; so he wrote a letter to the king of Israel and sent it with great gifts of money, jewels, and fine clothes. For, when the little girl had spoken of a prophet, Naaman never doubted that she meant the king.

When the king of Israel read the letter he was greatly disturbed. He knew that *he* could not cure leprosy and was afraid that Naaman was just looking for an excuse to attack the Hebrews.

Elisha, hearing how worried the king was, sent a message to him, saying, "Why do you worry? Let this Naaman come to me, and he shall know that there is a prophet in Israel."

So Naaman came with his horses and his chariot and stood at the door of the house of Elisha. Elisha did not come out himself, but sent a messenger to say, "Go and wash in the Jordan seven times, and your flesh will be healed and your leprosy gone."

Naaman was very angry and went away in a rage. "I surely thought the prophet himself would come out, that he would call on the name of the Lord his God, and that I should be well. There are rivers in Syria. Are they not so good as the rivers in Israel? May I not wash in *them* and be well?"

But his servants gathered about him and advised him to do as he had been told: "My lord, if the prophet had told you to do something very difficult, would you not have done it? How simple it is to do as he says, since we are so near the Jordan."

So they went down and Naaman dipped himself seven times in the Jordan. Just as Elisha had said, he was healed. Joyfully he returned to Elisha's house.

Standing before Elisha, Naaman said, "Now I know there is no God in all the earth but the God of Israel." He pressed gifts on Elisha, but Elisha would take nothing.

Then Naaman asked that Elisha give him some earth, as much as he could carry on two mules, so that he could take it back to Syria and build on it an altar to the God of Israel. He vowed he would worship no other gods. Then he departed.

When Naaman had gone, Gehazi, Elisha's servant, said to himself, "Behold—my master has saved Naaman this Syrian and has taken no gift or payment in return. I will run after him and get something."

So Gehazi followed. And when Naaman saw him running after him, he stopped his chariot, got down, and asked, "Is there something wrong?"

"All is well," answered Gehazi. "But my master has sent me to say he has changed his mind. Two young men, sons of the prophets, have arrived. Send them, I pray you, a talent of silver and two changes of garments."

Naaman sent back two servants with two talents of silver and fine garments. When they came to the house, Gehazi took the gifts and sent Naaman's servants away.

When Gehazi went in to his master, Elisha asked, "Where have you been, Gehazi?"

And Gehazi answered, "I have been nowhere."

So Elisha said, "I know you went after Naaman and took gifts of money and clothes. Therefore you and your descendants shall have Naaman's leprosy." And Gehazi went away a leper.

Under King Ahab the Israelites were troubled every-where. Robber bands came sweeping down from Syria to lay waste the flocks and fields. Each time the prophet Elisha warned the people. Then the Syrian king sent out horse-men and chariots to capture Elisha.

When the prophet's servant saw them coming, he cried: "O master, what shall we do?" But Elisha answered: "Fear not, for they that be with us are more than they that be with them." Then the eyes of the servant beheld that the mountain was full of chariots of fire round about Elisha. And as the prophet prayed, the Syrians became confused and lost their way, and wandered into the midst of the hosts of Israel.

Instead of ordering the invaders to be slain, Elisha per-suaded the ruler of Israel to place meat and drink before them and to let them go in peace. And they returned to their own land, and their robber bands came no more to trouble Israel.

King Ahab's death brought no relief to Israel, for his son, Joram, too, was a tyrant. And so the Prophet Elisha, with oil from the sacred horn, anointed young Jehu, son of Jehoshaphat, and the people of Israel accepted him as their king.

Immediately Jehu leaped into his chariot and drove furiously toward Jezreel. It chanced that a watchman on the wall of the city saw the dust from Jehu's chariot, and he warned King Joram.

Joram sprang into his own chariot and rode forth from the palace to meet the stranger. As the two chariots drew together, Jehu shouted: "I have come to punish you and your mother Jezebel for all the evil you have brought to our people." And drawing his bow with his full strength, he sent an arrow into Joram's heart. Then he ordered the king's body thrown to the dogs, and drove on to the palace.

When Jezebel learned of Jehu's approach, she painted her face and adorned her body and leaned out of her window, hoping to entice the man who had slain her son. But Jehu coldly ordered the eunuchs to hurl their wicked mistress down from the window, and she was dashed to death upon the stones of the street. And so was the house of Ahab destroyed and the word of the prophets fulfilled.

Joash, the Boy King

WHILE JORAM, SON OF AHAB, STILL WAS ruling in Samaria, Ahaziah came to the throne of Judah. Ahaziah's wickedness was as abominable as that of Ahab, for his mother, Athaliah, was his counselor and she was of the family of Ahab.

Ahaziah had reigned only one year when he was slain by his enemies.

When Athaliah learned that her son was dead, she saw an opportunity to rule over Judah herself. So she went to destroy all the royal princes, her own grandchildren, while they slept.

Now Ahaziah had a sister, Jehosheba, who wanted to prevent this. She stole into the chambers where the young princes were sleeping. She took away the baby Joash and his nurse, so that Joash alone, of all the king's sons, was not slain.

Jehosheba was married to Jehoiada, a priest of the temple, one of the few who were loyal to God. She took Joash to her husband, and he hid the child in the temple for six years, while Athaliah reigned over the land.

Jehoiada taught Joash of the God of Abraham and Isaac, the Lord of Israel. He kept a guard about the temple, and Athaliah never knew that Joash had been saved.

When Joash was thirteen years old, Jehoiada quietly sent trusted messengers throughout the kingdom to find those of the people who still were faithful to God and to bring them to the temple. When these people were gathered, he gave to their captains spears and shields which had belonged to King David and had been kept in the temple. He stationed all the people, every man having a weapon in his hand, about the temple and the altar.

The girl suggested that Naaman go to the prophet Elisha in Samaria. (Page 115)

Then he brought forth the young Prince, and made him king. (Page 121)

Then he brought forth the young prince, set the crown upon his head, and made him king. Jehoiada blessed him and said, "God save the king."

The people took up the cry and clapped their hands loudly. "God save the king!" The excitement grew, and people in the streets came running to know what was happening.

When Athaliah heard the noise of the people praising the newly crowned king, she ran to the temple. There between the pillars at the entrance she saw the young king. She saw the guards with their weapons and heard the trumpeters and the people rejoicing.

Tearing her clothes, she cried, "Treason! Treason!"

But the guards dragged her from the temple and killed her. The people broke down the temple of Baal and smashed his altar and images. Jehoiada made a covenant with the people, that Joash should be king and that they should serve the Lord.

Amidst great rejoicing and with singing, the guards and the nobles, the governors and all the people, brought Joash down from the temple and set him upon the throne of the kingdom.

Joash did what was right in the sight of God. He repaired the temple of the Lord, which had been greatly damaged during Athaliah's reign. He had a chest made and set it at the gate of the house of the Lord. All the princes and the people brought money and cast it into the chest and filled it over and over, and they hired masons and carpenters and repaired the temple. When they had finished, they brought the rest of the money and made gold and silver ornaments.

Every day, as long as Jehoiada lived, they offered burnt offerings in the house of the Lord. When Jehoiada grew old and died, he was buried in the City of David among the kings, because he had been faithful to Israel and toward God and the king.

After the death of Jehoiada, the nobles of Judah gathered near the king. They flattered him and gave him evil advice—to all of which he listened. Very soon they left the temple of the Lord and served idols—and Joash followed them. When Jehoiada's son warned the people that they would not prosper unless they followed the Lord, they stoned him and killed him.

At the end of that very year the armies of Syria came

against Jerusalem and the kingdom of Judah. They destroyed all the princes and took their riches back to their own treasure houses. The Lord did not help Joash. When they had left the land, Joash's own people turned against him and killed him. They buried him in the City of David but would not bury him among the kings, for he had turned against the Lord.

The Babylonian Invasion

ABOUT TWO HUNDRED YEARS AFTER THE death of Joash, his direct descendant Jehoiakim was ruling over Judah in Jerusalem. Like his fathers before him, he did that which was evil in the sight of the Lord.

Then Nebuchadnezzar, king of Babylon, came with a great army to besiege Jerusalem. They carried off the vessels of the Lord's temple and put them in his temple at Babylon, and bound the king of Judah in fetters and carried him off to Babylon. And Jehoiachin, son of the captured king, reigned in his stead over Judah.

Jehoiachin was no better than his father. And it was only three months before Nebuchadnezzar returned and besieged Jerusalem again. Jehoiachin went out and surrendered to Nebuchadnezzar—he and his mother, his servants, his princes and his officers.

Nebuchadnezzar carried away from Jerusalem all the treasures from the Lord's temple and the king's house. And he carried away ten thousand captives and all the craftsmen and smiths, and those who were strong and apt for war, so that none remained save the poorest of the people in the land. And Nebuchadnezzar placed Zedekiah, brother of Jehoiachin, to rule over the kingdom.

In the ninth year of his reign, Zedekiah rebelled against the king of Babylon. Then Nebuchadnezzar once more came with all his host against Jerusalem. He built forts round about the city and besieged it for two years, until famine prevailed and there was not even bread for the people.

Then one night Zedekiah and his men of war escaped through the city walls by way of a gate in the king's garden and fled toward the plains. But the enemy pursued him, scattered his army, and took him prisoner. They slew his sons before his eyes, then blinded him, bound him in chains, and carried him off to Babylon.

They burned the temple of the Lord, burned all the palaces within the city, and broke down the walls of Jerusalem. The rest of the people that were left in the city they carried away as slaves, and left only a few poor people to care for the vineyards and fields.

Thus was proud Jerusalem desolated, and her people scattered as chaff before the wind, because they had turned aside from the true God and had persisted in their wickedness.

Daniel

AMONG THE CHILDREN OF ISRAEL WHO HAD been carried off to Babylon there were four handsome, strong, and intelligent boys, children of the princes. They were Daniel, Hananiah, Michael, and Azariah.

By the order of King Nebuchadnezzar they were taught the Chaldean language and were given the same meat, provisions, and wine as were served the king, so that at the end of three years they might be ready to serve in the king's court. Their names were changed—Daniel's to Belteshazzar, Hananiah's to Shadrach, Mishael's to Meshach, and Azariah's to Abednego.

Daniel, who had been brought up in the way of the Lord, vowed to himself that he would not eat the meat and wine of the king—for they were not prepared according to the laws of Moses. Melzar, prince of the eunuchs, who had been put in charge of the boys, became very fond of Daniel. He said, "If you do not eat your meat and your drink you will grow thin and pale—and then my life will be in danger for not taking proper care of you."

Daniel's answer was: "Try for ten days. Give us herbs to eat and water to drink as we are used to have. Then compare us with those who eat of the king's meat."

At the end of the ten days, their faces were fairer and fatter than those of the others, so Melzar allowed them to continue.

God was with these four children and He gave them great knowledge and skill. Daniel had more understanding than the others and could interpret visions and dreams.

At the end of three years, all the Hebrew children were brought in to Nebuchadnezzar. He spoke with them and questioned them and found none like Belteshazzar, Shadrach, Meshach, and Abednego. He kept them in his court to serve him, and in all matters of wisdom and understanding he found them ten times wiser than all the magicians and astrologers in his kingdom.

Nebuchadnezzar's Dream

ONE NIGHT NEBUCHADNEZZAR HAD A dream that troubled him deeply. He called all his wise men, magicians, and astrologers to him. They said: "Tell us your dream, O king, and we will tell you the meaning of it."

But Nebuchadnezzar could not remember the dream. He threatened to kill the wise men if they failed to tell him both the dream and its meaning. They protested loudly that no king ever had asked such a thing before and that there was no magician, no sorcerer, no astrologer in all the kingdom who could do it.

The king was furious and ordered that all the wise men in Babylon be slain, and the guards searched for them throughout the land. When they came to Daniel, he wanted to know why the king had given such an order. When he heard the story, he went to the king and said that, given a little time, he would interpret the dream. The king agreed.

Daniel went home to his house to tell his three friends. They all prayed to God that He might recall to them the king's dream, and that night, in a vision, God revealed the secret to Daniel.

In the morning they thanked and praised God. Then Daniel went before the king and said, "The wise men cannot know the dream you had or what it means, but there is a God in heaven who can, and He has shown it to me.

"In your dream you saw a bright, terrible image. His head was of gold, his chest and arms were silver, his stomach and thighs brass, his legs and feet part of iron and part of clay.

"Then you saw a great stone thrown at his feet—and they were broken in pieces. When the feet broke all the rest, the gold, silver, and all, crumbled and was blown away in the wind. And nothing remained but the stone, which became a great mountain and filled the whole earth."

The king was amazed, for that had been his dream.

Then Daniel continued: "That was your dream, and now we shall tell you its meaning.

"God has given you power, strength and glory, and has made you a mighty ruler. You are the head of gold. After you there shall be lesser kingdoms. Those are the silver and the brass. Where you saw iron and clay, the kingdom shall be divided—partly strong and partly broken.

"In that day the divided kingdom shall not be left to other kings, but it shall be consumed. And God shall set up a kingdom which shall never be destroyed, and it shall stand forever."

Nebuchadnezzar was so amazed and impressed that he fell on his face before Daniel and said, "Truly your God is a great God, a Lord of kings and a revealer of secrets, since you were able to tell me all this."

In his gratitude he gave Daniel many rich gifts, and made him chief governor over all the wise men of Babylon.

The Fiery Furnace

SOME TIME LATER, NEBUCHADNEZZAR MADE a huge image of gold and set it up outside the city. Then he sent for all the princes and governors, the captains, the judges, the treasurers, the counselors, the sheriffs, and all the rulers of the provinces to come to the dedication of the image.

And when they and all the people were gathered together, a herald cried aloud, "To you it is commanded that when you shall hear the sound of music, you shall all fall down and worship the golden image. Whosoever does not, shall in the same hour be cast into a fiery furnace."

When the people heard the music they all bowed down and worshiped the image—all except Shadrach, Meshach, and Abednego, the three friends of Daniel. They were brought before the king, but they still refused to worship his golden image.

Nebuchadnezzar, enraged, ordered that the furnace be heated seven times hotter than usual and that they be bound and thrown in. It was so hot that the flames which shot out the door burned to death those men who had cast them into the fire.

Then the king was filled with wonder, for on looking into the furnace, he saw that the bonds of the prisoners were loose, that they were walking about unhurt, and that an angel seemed to be with them. So he called to them, and they came out. Not even a hair of their heads had been singed, nor had their clothes been scorched.

Nebuchadnezzar blessed their God and made a decree: That all who spoke against the God of the Hebrews should be cut in pieces and their houses destroyed, for there was no other god who could deliver his people in such a way. Then he promoted Shadrach, Meshach, and Abednego to high offices in the province of Babylon.

The Humbling of Nebuchadnezzar

AS NEBUCHADNEZZAR'S KINGDOM BECAME rich and powerful, the king's pride and arrogance grew. He thought nothing could take his power from him.

One night he dreamed a strange dream, and in the morning called Daniel before him to interpret it. In this dream he saw a great branching, flourishing tree. And a voice came, saying: "Cut down the branches and hew them to pieces, leaving only the stump. Let it be wet with dew, and change its heart from that of a man to that of a beast until seven times have passed."

Daniel was troubled. It was an hour before he answered: "O king, you will not like the interpretation of this dream, but your enemies will rejoice in it. It means that in your arrogance and strength you have sinned much, and therefore you will be humbled and driven from your palace to live in the fields like a beast. However, after seven years, you will repent and be restored to your throne."

One year later Nebuchadnezzar lost his reason, and his people drove him from his throne. He lived in the fields eating grass as the beasts do, until his hair grew like eagles' feathers, and his nails like the claws of a bear.

After seven years his reason returned, and he became king again, even as Daniel had said, and thereafter ruled more mercifully and justly.

Belshazzar's Feast

AFTER NEBUCHADNEZZAR'S DEATH, HIS SON Belshazzar succeeded him. When the young man came to the throne, he gave a great feast for all the nobles and lords. While they were drinking wine, he ordered that the gold and silver vessels which his father had taken from the temple in Jerusalem be brought. In these wine was served, and while the guests drank, they praised their gods and idols of gold and silver, and wood and stone.

But suddenly when the revelry was at its height there appeared the fingers of a man's hand writing strange words on the palace wall before the throng. The music and the laughter ceased. The king grew pale, and his knees trembled so violently that they knocked together.

Immediately he cried aloud for his wise men and said, "Whosoever shall read this writing and tell me its meaning shall be clothed in royal scarlet, have a chain of gold about his neck, and be third ruler in the kingdom."

But none of the wise men could even read the writing.

Then Belshazzar's wife remembered Daniel, whom Nebuchadnezzar had made governor of the wise men, and his power to interpret dreams. So they called Daniel, and he spoke.

"Let your gifts and rewards be given to another; yet I will read the writing and make known its interpretation.

An angel guarded Daniel so the lions would not hurt him. (Page 134)

The three wise men brought precious gifts. (Page 147)

"You have not profited by your father's experience: you have drunk wine from the sacred vessels of God's temple: you have praised gods and images of gold, silver, iron, wood, and stone, which see not, nor hear nor know; yet you have not glorified God, Who holds your very breath in His hand.

"The fingers of the hand were sent from God. The writing that was written is MENE, MENE, TEKEL, UPHARSIN, and it means: God has numbered the days of your kingdom. You have been weighed in the balances and found wanting. Your kingdom shall be divided and given to the Medes and Persians."

Belshazzar did as he had promised. Daniel was clothed in royal scarlet, a chain of gold was put about his neck, and he was made third ruler in the kingdom.

Yet in that very night Belshazzar, king of Babylon and the Chaldeans, was slain. Darius, the young ruler of the Medes and the Persians, took over the kingdom.

Daniel in the Lion's Den

NOW THE KINGDOM OF DARIUS WAS LARGE. There were one hundred and twenty princes ruled over by three presidents, of whom Daniel was first. All the princes gave their accounting to him, and he saw that the king was not cheated, for he was very fair and just.

The princes were jealous of Daniel, but because he was so faithful to the king, they could find no fault with him—and no way to get rid of him.

They decided they could never find anything against him except his worship of God. So they persuaded the king to sign a decree declaring that anyone who prayed to any god or man except Darius should be cast into a den of lions.

Darius was pleased, and never thinking of Daniel and how he prayed to God every day, he signed the decree.

Even though he knew that the decree had been signed, Daniel went home, knelt before his open windows which faced toward Jerusalem, and prayed and gave thanks to God just as he had always done.

The jealous nobles saw him. They went straight to the king and asked, "Did you not sign a decree saying that anyone who made a petition of any god within thirty days should be cast into the den of lions?"

The king replied, "That is true, according to the law of the Medes and Persians, which cannot be changed."

Instantly they answered, "Daniel, the captive from Judah, pays no attention, but makes his petitions to his God three times a day."

Then Darius was angry, for he saw the trap which the nobles had set. All day he tried to think of a way to save

Daniel, whom he loved and respected and whom he knew he could trust.

But when evening came the nobles returned to tell the king what he knew very well. "The law of the Medes and Persians is that no decree signed by the king may be changed."

So the king commanded that Daniel be put into the lions' den. The mouth of the den was closed with a stone, and the king sealed it himself. But he said to Daniel, "Your God, whom you serve so faithfully, will surely deliver you."

Then Darius returned to his palace. He made the musicians put away their instruments, and he neither ate nor slept.

Very early in the morning he went in haste to the lions' den.

"O Daniel," he cried out, "has your God saved you from the lions?"

And then he heard Daniel's voice in answer, "O king, live for ever! My God has sent His angel, who has closed the lions' mouths so that they have not hurt me, for He knows I have done no wrong."

Then with great joy Darius ordered that Daniel be taken from the den, and commanded that those men who had accused Daniel be cast into the den in his stead, and the lions ate them.

Then King Darius issued a decree stating that in all

parts of his kingdom men were to worship the God of
Daniel from that day forth.

Queen Esther

IN THE THIRD YEAR OF THE REIGN OF KING
Ahasuerus over Persia and Media, the king invited all
his princes and servants to a magnificent feast.

Now while he was merry with wine, he ordered his
chamberlains to bring Queen Vashti, with the royal crown,
to show her great beauty to the princes and the people.
But the queen refused to come before the strangers.

Then his wise men advised Ahasuerus to banish his wife.
They reasoned that she had wronged the king by not obey-
ing his command and that she had insulted his guests.
Likewise, if the women of Persia and Media were to hear
that such disobedience had gone unpunished, they would
have nothing but contempt for their husbands forever-
more.

So the king issued a decree that every man should be
ruler in his own house and that the wives should give
honor and obedience to their husbands.

Then all the fair young women of the kingdom were
brought before the king so that he might choose a new
queen.

Now there was in the capital, Shushan, a certain Jew named Mordecai, who had been carried away a captive from Jerusalem during the Babylonian invasion. He had adopted and brought up Esther, his uncle's daughter, for she was an orphan. She was fair and beautiful. Mordecai warned her not to disclose her race when she was brought before the king.

The king, seeing Esther, loved her above all the others, and he set the royal crown on her head and made her queen instead of Vashti.

Mordecai went every day to the king's gate and walked beneath the queen's window in the palace of the women, hoping that he might hear news of his adopted daughter. One day he overheard two of the king's chamberlains plotting to kill the king.

He warned Esther, who told the king. When the treachery was investigated, and the plot exposed, the two men were caught and hanged, and the heart of King Ahasuerus was filled with gratitude toward Mordecai.

Haman's Plan to Destroy the Jews

ONE OF THE CHIEF PRINCES OF THE KINGdom of the Medes and Persians was Haman. All the king's servants except Mordecai bowed low before him as he entered the king's gate. This so enraged the proud Prince Haman that he determined to destroy not only Mordecai but all of the Jews who were in the whole kingdom of Ahasuerus.

Accordingly, he persuaded the king to give him his royal signet ring, and then sent letters sealed with the king's seal to the governors of all the provinces of Persia, ordering them on a certain day to slay every man, woman, and child of Jewish blood, and to confiscate their belongings.

As soon as Mordecai learned what Haman had done, he put on sackcloth and ashes and cried with a loud and bitter cry before the king's gate.

When Queen Esther heard of it, she bade Mordecai gather all the Jews in Shushan to fast and pray for three days. Then, against the law (for the king had not summoned her), she put on her royal garments and went in to Ahasuerus.

When the king saw Esther standing modestly in his court, near his throne, instead of being angry, he held out his golden scepter to her, and said, "What is your request, Queen Esther? Though it be half my kingdom, it shall be given to you."

And Esther asked only that the king and Haman come to the banquet she would prepare for them the next day.

Haman was joyful, and went home to tell his family how

he had been honored not only by the king but now by the queen as well. But on the way he had passed Mordecai, who still refused to bow to him. So his joy turned to anger and he ordered a gallows to be built fifty cubits high upon which the stubborn Mordecai was to be hanged.

Esther Saves Her People

THAT NIGHT THE KING COULD NOT SLEEP, and he called for the book of chronicles to be read to him. When he heard that Mordecai once had uncovered a plot against his life, Ahasuerus said, "What honor was done to Mordecai for this?" And his servants answered, "Nothing."

The next morning Haman came to the king's court to discuss the hanging of Mordecai. But before he could speak, the king asked him, "What shall be done for a man whom the king wishes to honor?"

Haman thought the king was referring to him, so he answered, "Let him be arrayed in royal garments and led on horseback through the streets of the city, while it is proclaimed that he is so honored by the king." Great was Haman's discomfiture when he heard the king say: "So let it be done to Mordecai, for once he saved my life." And there was black hatred in Haman's heart when he came to the queen's banquet.

Here the king asked Esther what was her petition.

Then Esther said, "If it please the king, let my life be given me and my people. For we are to perish, I and my people—to be slain and destroyed by an enemy."

Then the king cried out, "Who and where is he that dares to do such a thing?"

And Esther said, "The enemy is this wicked Haman."

Then Haman was afraid, for he saw that the king was weighing evil in his mind against him.

Just then a chamberlain came and told of the gallows Haman had built for Mordecai. The king said, "Hang Haman thereon instead."

So they hanged Haman on the gallows he had prepared for Mordecai. Ahasuerus spared all the Jews, and Haman's worldly goods were divided among Queen Esther's people.

Job

THERE WAS IN THE LAND OF UZ A MAN whose name was Job. He was good and very rich, with great flocks of sheep and goats and herds of camels and asses, and with seven sons and three daughters and many servants. And because of his blameless life, God thought very highly of Job.

Now Satan, who had often heard Jehovah speak of His servant Job with pride in his uprightness, sought to change His mind. He went before Jehovah and urged that the man of Uz be put to the test of losing all his worldly goods.

So Jehovah agreed to put His servant to the test.

One day soon after, a messenger came to tell Job that his oxen and asses and servants had been set upon by the Sabeans and that he alone had escaped death or capture.

While he was yet speaking, another servant came in to say that all Job's sheep and those guarding them had been consumed by fire. And another came to report that the Chaldeans had stolen Job's camels.

Before he had finished there came one last servant to say, "Your sons and daughters were all eating in their eldest brother's house, when a great wind came from the wilderness. It smote all four corners of the house at once, and the house was destroyed, and all the children and servants were killed."

Then Job arose, tearing his clothes in grief. He shaved his head, fell to the ground, and worshiped God, saying, "The Lord gave, and now the Lord has taken away. Blessed be the name of the Lord."

Then the Lord said to Satan, "Although you have afflicted him without cause, there still is none so good on the earth as my servant Job."

But Satan argued, "A man will give all he has to save his life. But touch his bone or flesh and he will curse You."

And the Lord said, "He is in your power, only save his life."

So Satan smote Job with sore boils from the sole of his foot to the crown of his head. Then Job's wife, in despair, came to the city gate where Job sat in the dust scraping his sores with a piece of broken pottery, and said to him, "Curse God, and die." But Job answered, "You speak like a foolish woman. We receive good from the hand of the Lord. Shall we not therefore also receive evil?"

Job's friends came and mourned and argued with him, but still Job would not raise his voice against the Lord.

At last God, knowing that Job would be faithful to the end, saw that it was needless to test him further. Job had remained true to his faith against all of the temptations and trials devised by Satan, so God rewarded him twofold in worldly goods, and the remainder of Job's days were full of peace and contentment.

Jonah

SOME FEW CENTURIES BEFORE THE BIRTH of Jesus, there came out of Galilee a prophet named Jonah whom the Lord commanded to go to preach before the wicked inhabitants of the city of Nineveh.

But Jonah, afraid to go to a strange city alone and preach against the people, thought to escape the task the Lord had commanded him to do. He fled in the opposite direction, to Joppa, on the coast. There he found a boat going to Tarshish. He paid his fare, boarded the boat, and went inside to sleep.

But the Lord sent a mighty tempest, so violent that the boat was in danger of being broken up. The sailors were terrified. They threw the cargo overboard and cried out to their gods, but nothing availed. Then they cast lots to find out who was to blame for this evil that had come to them, and the lot fell upon Jonah.

Jonah told them how he had fled the Lord. He added, "It is because of me that this tempest has descended upon you. Throw me into the sea, and the waves will be calmed."

Nevertheless the men tried to row the boat to shore to save Jonah. When they could not move against the storm, they cried to the Lord, "Let us not perish for this man's life. This is not our will but Yours," and they took Jonah up and cast him into the sea. And the tempest abated and the waves became calm.

But Jonah did not drown. Jehovah caused a great whale to swim near, and the whale swallowed Jonah. For three days and nights Jonah remained in the whale's belly, repenting of his folly and praying to the Lord.

After the third day the whale cast Jonah up on the shore. Now Jonah obeyed the voice of the Lord and hastened to Nineveh. As soon as he had entered the gates of the wicked city, he began to declare that unless the people mended their ways, in forty days they would all be destroyed, and their city as well.

And the people of Nineveh heeded the warning of Jonah, and God spared them and their city.

Joseph took the infant Boy and His mother in the night, and departed. (Page 148)

They found Him talking with the most learned men of the synagogue. (Page 149)

The New Testament

Jesus is Born

FIVE CENTURIES CAME AND WENT BE-
tween the time of the last events chronicled in the
Old Testament and the birth of Jesus, with which the New
Testament opens. They were turbulent years for the children of Israel. Palestine changed hands many times until,
finally, it became a part of the Roman Empire under Au-
gustus Caesar, with Herod as King of Judea.

There lived at that time, in the city of Nazareth in Galilee, a virgin named Mary. To her the angel of the Lord
appeared in a vision, saying: "Blessed art thou among
women, for the Lord is with thee: thou shalt bring forth a
Son and shall call His name Jesus. He shall become King of
Kings, and of His reign there shall be no end, for He is
the Son of God." And Mary, who had feared at first, was
filled with a great joy.

Some time later, the Emperor having ordered all of the
people of his empire to go each to his own city to be taxed,
Joseph took his wife Mary to his native Bethlehem, nearly
a hundred miles away.

When they came to the end of their long journey, they found the inn crowded. Since there was no room, they were compelled to go out into the stable where the cattle were. And there, in a manger, Jesus was born. Mary wrapped Him in swaddling clothes, and laid Him gently in the straw.

In the same country that night there were shepherds guarding their flocks, and to them the angel of the Lord appeared and a great light shone in the sky. The humble shepherds were afraid, but the angel said to them: "Fear not: for I bring you good tidings of great joy. For this day a Savior is born to all the world." Suddenly with the angel there was a heavenly multitude, praising God and saying: "Glory to God in the Highest, and on earth peace, good will toward men."

Then the shepherds arose and went into Bethlehem and to the stable, where they found Mary and the Child. And as they kneeled before the Christ-child, again they heard angel voices singing: "Peace on earth, good will toward men."

The Three Wise Men

ON THE NIGHT THAT JESUS WAS BORN, three wise men came riding on camels out of the East into Jerusalem. "Where is He that is the new-born

King of the Jews?" they asked. "We have seen His star in the East and have come to worship Him."

King Herod was greatly disturbed, for he feared that a new ruler would rise up and overthrow him. Anxiously he questioned his high priests: "What do the prophets say of this?" They replied: "It is written that the Child shall be born in Bethlehem."

So Herod ordered the wise men to find the Babe, and when they did so to send for him so that he, also, might worship. And the star which they had seen in the East went before them and led them to the place where Mary and Jesus were, in the stable of the inn.

There they fell down before Him and worshiped. Opening their treasures, they spread before the Child precious gifts of gold and frankincense and myrrh.

Flight into Egypt

BEING WARNED BY GOD NOT TO RETURN to Herod and reveal where the future King lay, the wise men returned to their country by another route.

Then an angel appeared to Joseph in a dream, saying, "Arise, take the young Child and His mother and flee to Egypt. Herod fears for his throne and is searching for the

Babe to kill Him. Remain in Egypt until I bring you word that it is safe to return."

Then Joseph rose up and took the infant Boy and His mother in the night, and departed into Egypt.

When Herod discovered that the wise men had not returned, he was greatly enraged, and still more afraid he might lose his throne. So he sent his soldiers to Bethlehem and all the neighboring towns with orders to kill all the baby boys who were two years old and under. In this way, he felt sure he could rid himself of this new King who, according to the prophecy, was to rule over Israel and the world. But the Babe was now safe in Egypt.

When Herod died, the angel of the Lord appeared again to Joseph and told him it was safe to return to Israel. So they set out for Jerusalem. But as they neared the city they heard that Herod's son Archelaus was ruling in his father's stead. Joseph was still fearful, so they turned aside and went to Nazareth to make their home. Jesus grew strong in body and mind.

The Passover Feast

EVERY YEAR, AT THE FEAST OF THE PASS-over, Joseph and Mary went to Jerusalem. Here they offered sacrifices to God, in memory of the night He killed all the first-born in Egypt but passed over the Hebrews. When Jesus was twelve years old, His parents took Him with them on their pilgrimage to Jerusalem.

When the feast was over and Joseph and Mary started on the return journey to Nazareth, they suddenly became aware that Jesus was not with them. Since there was a crowd of people traveling together, Joseph and Mary supposed the Boy to be with some of their friends and kinsfolk scattered throughout the long caravan. But when they stopped that night and did not find Him, they were very worried and returned to Jerusalem to look for Him.

They searched for three days without finding Him. Finally they went to the temple and there they found the Boy quietly and earnestly talking with the most learned men of the synagogue.

All who heard Him were astonished at His wisdom and understanding. Even His parents were amazed. But, motherlike, Mary said to Him, "Son, why did You stay behind? Your father and I have been looking anxiously for You everywhere."

Calmly Jesus answered, "Why is it that you looked for Me? Did you not know that I must be about My Father's business?"

Mary and Joseph could not understand what He meant. But Jesus went back to Nazareth with them and was a good son, and obeyed their wishes until He grew to manhood.

The Baptism of Jesus

THE YEARS PASSED QUIETLY IN NAZARETH. But when Jesus was about thirty years of age, the people began to hear of the preaching of an Elijah-like young prophet in the desert wilderness to the south. Dressed in his camel's-hair robe with a leathern girdle about his waist, he presented a strange appearance, but so fiery was his tongue that all the people, even as far as the Jordan, went out into the wilderness to hear him preach and, having confessed their sins, to be baptized. When the Jews sent priests from Jerusalem to ask the fiery preacher who he was, the preacher, whose name was John, answered, "I am not the Christ."

Then they said to him, "Who are you, that we may bring an answer to those who sent us?"

And John made answer, "I am the voice of one crying in the wilderness. Make straight the way of the Lord, as said the prophet Isaiah."

Then they asked him, "If you are neither Christ, nor a prophet, why do you baptize?"

John answered them, "I baptize with water. But there stands One among you whom you know not. He it is Who, coming after me, is preferred before me, the strings of Whose shoes I am not good enough to untie."

One day Jesus came with the crowds to the Jordan, and asked that John baptize Him too. The hermit, astonished, answered, "It is rather You who should baptize me." But Jesus insisted, and they came from the water, praying, heaven opened and the spirit of God descended on Jesus in the form of a dove. And a voice came from heaven saying, "This is My beloved Son, in Whom I am well pleased."

Then Jesus went into the wilderness, as had Moses, to fast for forty days and nights, to pray and talk with God.

And when the fast was over, and Jesus was hungry, Satan came and said to Him: "If you are indeed the Son of God, command that these stones become bread!"

But Jesus answered: "It is written that man shall not live by bread alone, but by the word of God."

Then the devil took Him to the pinnacle of the temple in the holy city, and there tempted Jesus for a second time: "If You are the Son of God, cast Yourself down from this height, and the angels will bear You up in their hands."

Jesus refused, saying, "It is written again, you shall not tempt the Lord your God."

Satan tempted Him a third time. He carried Him on to a high mountain and showed Him all the kingdoms of the earth and their glory. "These shall be Yours, if You will fall down and worship me."

But Jesus answered: "Get you far from Me, Satan, for it is written, you shall worship the Lord God, and Him only shall you serve."

Then the devil went, and angels ministered to Jesus.

The First Disciples

FILLED WITH THE POWER OF THE SPIRIT, Jesus returned from the wilderness to the scene of His baptism where John still labored. He went about all Galilee, preaching in the synagogues, and the people were amazed because He taught them with authority, confirming His words with all manner of healings.

Once as he was passing the lake of Gennesaret, He saw two fishing boats upon the shore. He said to Simon and Andrew, the two brothers who owned them: "Launch the ship and fish." Discouraged, they answered: "Master, we have toiled all through the night and have caught nothing."

Nevertheless, obedient to His word, they let down their nets once more over the side of their boat. When they tried to pull the nets in, they found them too heavy with fishes to be lifted. And when they tried to thank Him, Jesus said: "Follow Me and I will make you fishers of men." So Simon and Andrew became His first disciples.

Soon afterward they were joined by James and John, his brother, who, too, were fishermen. And as they continued along the way, Jesus called to Matthew, a tax-gatherer, who was sitting at the customs gate, "Follow Me," and Matthew joined the five. Then Jesus found Philip, who brought with him Nathaniel. Soon the band of disciples numbered twelve in all—Simon, called Peter, Andrew, James, John, Philip, Bartholomew, Thomas, Matthew, James (son of Alphaeus), Thaddeus, Simon the Canaanite, and Judas Iscariot.

The Wine for the Wedding

ONE OF THE EARLY MIRACLES PERFORMED by Jesus took place at Cana in Galilee at a wedding feast to which Jesus, Mary, His mother, and His disciples were invited guests.

In the middle of the feast it was discovered that the wine had given out. Knowing that failure of wine for the feast would disgrace her host, Mary came to Jesus and said, "Alas, they have no wine." To the servants she whispered: "No matter what strange thing He asks of you, do it."

Now there stood near the banquet table six huge stone water-jars such as the servants used in washing clothes. Jesus said: "Fill these water-jars with water." And the servants filled them to the brim. Then He commanded them: "Draw out some now and carry it to the master of the feast."

The servants bore the liquid wonderingly to the ruler of the feast at the head of the table. When he had tasted of it, he called to the bridegroom: "Others serve their best wine first at the feast, and afterward, when men's appetites are dulled, they bring forth the poorest quality. But you have saved the best wine till now!"

So, from the disgrace of inhospitality Jesus saved his friends. And His disciples saw what He had done and they believed in Him.

The Samaritan Woman

ON HIS RETURN TO GALILEE, JESUS HAD TO pass through the province of Samaria. When He reached the little Samaritan city of Sychar, He paused to rest at noonday by a well, known as Jacob's Well because, many years before, the piece of ground where the water sprang forth had been given by Jacob to his son Joseph.

And as He rested there, a woman of Samaria came with a jar to draw water from the well. Jesus said: "Give Me some water to drink." Surprised, the woman replied: "How is it that you, a Jew, ask a drink of me, a Samaritan? For the Jews look with contempt upon my people."

But Jesus answered: "If you but knew Who it is that asks for a drink, you would ask it of Him instead, and He would give you living water, and you would never thirst again."

And as the Master talked with her, the woman of

Samaria forgot her bitterness, and she marveled at this strange Jew who had no hatred for anyone.

"I see you are a prophet," she said. Then she left the well, forgetting her water-jar, and entered the city calling: "I have seen the true Messiah!"

The Man at the Pool

AT THE TIME OF THE PASSOVER, JESUS WENT up to Jerusalem. Now in that city by the sheep market there was a pool fed by intermittent springs which was called Bethesda, because of its five porches. Great numbers of sick folk lay in these porches, waiting for the moving of the waters, for they believed that at certain times an angel came to trouble the waters, and that at such a time whosoever stepped first into the pool would be healed.

As Jesus came that way (it was on the Sabbath day) He saw a man lying there who had been a cripple for many years. "Would you like to be made whole?" He asked. And the cripple answered: "Sir, I have no one, when the water is troubled, to put me into the pool, for while I am coming, another steps in before me."

Then Jesus said: "Take up your bed and walk." Immediately the man was made well, and he walked.

When word of this healing reached the priests, they

"Follow Me and I will make you fishers of men." (Page 153)

Straightway the girl arose from her couch and walked. (Page 159)

charged Jesus with breaking the Sabbath. "My Father has worked till now, and I work," was His reply. This claim of equality with God the Jews hailed as blasphemy, and in the days to come it was the charge upon which Jesus was to be condemned.

The Sabbath Day

AS THE PHARISEES (THEY WERE THE RITUAL-ists among the Jews) beheld the people following after Jesus and proclaiming Him the Savior, they were filled with hatred and envy. They sought continually to find some accusation or blame against Him. And again and again they accused Him of breaking the Sabbath day.

One Sabbath, Jesus entered the synagogue to preach. There was a man with a withered hand, and as the Master paused before him, the Pharisees stood around to see whether Jesus would heal on the Sabbath day. Reading their thoughts, Jesus said to the man with the withered hand: "Stand forth." And he did so.

Then Jesus turned to the Pharisees and said: "Is it lawful on the Sabbath day to do good or to do evil, to save life or to destroy it? What man is there among you who shall have a sheep fall into a pit on the Sabbath, yet will not lift it out? Is not a man of greater value than a sheep? The Sabbath is made for man, not man for the Sabbath!"

Turning again to the man, He commanded: "Stretch forth your hand!" And the hand became whole.

Then the Pharisees withdrew and took counsel with the followers of Herod, seeking ways to destroy this man who always discomfited them. But Jesus passed safely through their midst, and went His way.

The Daughter of Jairus

ONE DAY WHILE JESUS WAS PREACHING BY the sea, with many people gathered about Him, one of the rulers of the synagogue, Jairus, came to Him. When he saw Jesus he fell at His feet and said, "My little daughter lies at the point of death. I beg You to come, lay Your hands on her that she may be cured. Then she shall live."

Jesus went with him, and having heard what Jairus asked, many people followed to see what would take place.

Among the crowds along the way, there was a woman who had been sick for a number of years. She had spent all her money trying to be cured and had seen many physicians, but she steadily grew worse. When she heard that Jesus was passing, she pushed through the crowd that was following Him, saying to herself, "If I can only touch His garments, I shall be cured." As she touched His garment, she immediately felt better and knew that she was cured.

Jesus, feeling that something had happened, turned in the crowd and said, "Who touched My clothes?"

His disciples, not knowing what had happened, answered, "You see this great crowd all about You and yet You ask who touched You?"

But the woman, now afraid, although she knew she was cured, came up and told Him what she had done. And He said to her, "Daughter, your faith has healed you. Go in peace, for you are well."

While He was still speaking, a messenger came from Jairus' house saying, "Your daughter is dead. Why trouble the Master any further?"

Jesus, hearing the man, said to Jairus, "Be not afraid, only believe."

When He came to the house of the ruler of the synagogue, He saw many people weeping and wailing. He said to them, "Why do you weep? The little girl is not dead, she is only sleeping." And they laughed Him to scorn.

But when He had put them all out, He took the father and mother, Peter, James, and John who were with Him, and went into the room where the little girl was lying. He took her by the hand and said, "Talitha cumi"—which means, "Damsel, I say to you, arise!"

Straightway the little girl arose from her couch and

walked. Jesus told them to give her something to eat and to tell no one what had happened.

And great was the astonishment at the power of Jesus, when all beheld that the daughter of Jairus was again alive and well.

A Prophet in His Own Country

WHEN JESUS HAD BEEN PREACHING FOR A long time in various cities, His thoughts turned back longingly to His own countryside where He had spent the days of His youth.

So one Sabbath day found Jesus back in His own Nazareth, preaching to His old townspeople in the synagogue. They began to whisper to one another:

"Is not this the carpenter, the son of Mary? Are not His brothers and His sisters living right here among us? Why does this carpenter set Himself up to teach us? What is this wisdom that has been given Him?"

And Jesus was sad when He saw His own people's lack of faith in Him. "Verily," He said, "a prophet is not without honor, save in his own country and among his own kin and in his own city."

And while He stayed in Nazareth He performed but few works of healing, so great was the people's unbelief.

The Man Born Blind

AGAIN ON A SABBATH DAY, AS JESUS WALKED with His disciples, He saw, sitting by the roadside, a man who had been born blind.

The disciples asked Him: "Master, who did sin, this man or his parents, that he was born blind?" And Jesus answered: "Neither he nor his parents have sinned. But the works of God shall be manifested in him."

Then He spat upon the ground, and making clay with the spittle, He anointed the man's eyes, saying: "Go, wash in the pool of Siloam." The man went his way, washing as he had been told, and when he returned, he could see as well as any other man.

His neighbors, scarcely believing, asked: "Is this really the blind man, or one who looks like him?" But the man answered: "I am he." And the Pharisees said among themselves: "This Jesus is not of God, for he breaks the Sabbath. Yet how could a sinner work such miracles?"

So they sought out the man who had been blind. They said: "Surely you do not think this Jesus, a sinner, has wrought the miracle. Give God the praise for your healing."

The man answered: "Whether He is a sinner or no, I know not. One thing I do know—that whereas I was blind, now I see!"

The House Built on the Rock

JESUS WENT WITH HIS DISCIPLES UP ONTO A mountain where He taught them: "Men shall be known by the fruits they bear. A good tree does not bring forth corrupt fruit. A thorn tree does not bear figs, nor a bramble-bush grapes. A good man, out of the treasure of his heart, brings forth good, and an evil man brings forth evil. So call Me not 'Master! Master!' unless you are prepared to do what I have taught you to do.

"If you hear My words, and follow them in your lives, then you are like a wise man who built his house upon a rock. And the rains fell, and the floods came, and the winds blew, and beat upon that house, but it fell not, for it was founded upon a rock.

"But he who listens to My words, and fails to obey them, is like a foolish man who built his house on the shifting sands. The rains fell, and the floods came, and the winds blew, and beat upon that house, and it fell, and great was the fall of it."

The Good Samaritan

ONE DAY A LAWYER, SEEKING TO TEST Jesus, said to Him, "Master, what shall I do to inherit eternal life?"

Jesus answered, "What is written in the law?"

The lawyer answered, from the laws which God had given to Moses on Mt. Sinai so many years before, "You shall love the Lord your God with all your heart, with all your soul, with all your strength and with all your mind. And you shall love your neighbor as yourself."

Jesus said, "That is exactly right. Do these things and you shall live."

But the lawyer said, "Yes, but who is my neighbor that I shall love?"

In answer, Jesus told him this story:—

"A certain man was traveling from Jerusalem to Jericho. A band of thieves fell upon him. They robbed him of all he had, took his clothes and his valuables, beat him, and left him half-dead by the roadside.

"By chance a priest was passing that way. When he saw the wounded man he passed by on the other side. Likewise a Levite who was traveling on the same road stopped and looked at the wounded stranger, and then he, too, went on.

"But a certain Samaritan, as he journeyed, came to the place. When he saw the wounded man, he stopped and went over to him. Filled with compassion, He poured oil on his wounds and bandaged them and gave him a little wine to drink to restore him. Then the Samaritan set the man upon his own beast, brought him to a near-by inn, and cared for him.

"The next day, before going on his way, the Samaritan left some money with the innkeeper, saying, 'Take care of this man. If you spend more than this, I will repay you the next time I pass.'

"Now," said Jesus to the lawyer, "which of these three travelers was a neighbor to the man who was robbed and beaten?"

Naturally, the lawyer answered: "The Samaritan, who had mercy on him." And this was a lesson in neighborliness that he never forgot.

Martha, Mary, and Lazarus

IT CAME TO PASS, AS JESUS WENT ON HIS WAY, that He entered the village of Bethany. A certain woman named Martha received Him into her house.

Martha busied herself about the house, preparing to serve Jesus and the disciples, but Mary, her sister, sat at Jesus' feet and listened to His words.

Then Martha went to Jesus and said, "My Lord, do You not care that my sister has left me to serve alone? Bid her to help me."

Jesus answered, "Martha, Martha—you are troubled about so many things, which really do not matter. In life there is only one thing necessary, and Mary has found it. And never shall it be taken away from her."

Jesus went on to Jerusalem—where a message from Martha and Mary in Bethany awaited Him, saying that Lazarus, their brother, and the beloved friend of the Master, lay grievously ill.

For two days Jesus stayed where He was. Then He said to His disciples, "Let us go to Bethany in Judea again." The disciples reminded Jesus that the last time he had been near Jerusalem, the Jews had sought to stone Him, and they did not want Him to go again.

Jesus only said, "Our friend Lazarus sleeps. But I go that I may awaken him."

Then His disciples said, "But Lord, if he sleeps, surely he will get well," for they thought Jesus meant that Lazarus was resting.

Now Jesus spoke more plainly, "Lazarus is dead. I am glad for your sakes that I was not there, that you may believe. Now let us go to him."

When they arrived in Bethany, they found many people there, come to comfort Martha and Mary because of their brother's death. Lazarus already had been in his tomb four days.

Both Martha and Mary, weeping, said to Jesus, "Lord, if only You had been here, our brother would not have died."

When Jesus saw them weeping and saw all the mourners, He too wept and asked, "Where have you laid him?"

They led Jesus to the cave where Lazarus had been buried, and rolled back the stone at the opening as He commanded.

Then Jesus lifted up His eyes and said, "Father, I thank You that You have heard me. I know that You hear me always, but because of the people who stand by, I call on You so that they may believe that You have sent me."

When He had spoken thus, He cried with a loud voice, "Lazarus, come forth!"

And Lazarus came forth, bound hand and foot with grave-clothes and his face bound about with a napkin.

Jesus said to them, "Loose him, and let him go."

Then many of the Jews who had come to comfort Martha and Mary at last believed Jesus to be the Messiah. As word went forth of the great miracle he had wrought in Bethany, the Pharisees and chief priests consulted together. They feared that if Jesus were allowed to go on performing miracles, all men would follow Him.

The Parable of the Seeds

ONE DAY JESUS WENT OUT AND SAT BY THE lake of Gennesaret, and great crowds of people gathered about, eager to hear Him. Now there were two fishing boats anchored near the shore, and Jesus stepped into one of them that belonged to Simon. Then He asked Simon to put off from shore a little, and He sat down and spoke to the people from the ship. He told them this story:

"Once a man went out to sow seed. Some seeds fell by the wayside and the birds ate them. Some fell on stony places where there was very little earth. They were scorched by the sun and died because they had almost no roots. Some fell among weeds where there was no room to grow. But many fell on good ground, and they grew and bore fruit, some a little, some more, and some a great deal."

Then His disciples asked, "Why do you speak in parables? Why do you not explain?"

Jesus explained:

"The sower sows the word of God. Those seeds sown by the wayside are the people who hear the word, but immediately Satan comes and takes the teaching from them.

"Those seeds sown on stony ground are such as hear the word and receive the teaching at first with joy, but as soon as afflictions come, forsake it.

"Those sown among the thorns are they who hear the teaching but who let the worldly pleasures of life choke it into unfruitfulness.

"But the seeds sown on good ground are those who hear the word and remember it, and live uprightly. And they bear fruit, sometimes thirtyfold, sometimes sixtyfold, sometimes an hundredfold."

The Death of John the Baptist

DURING ALL THIS TIME THE FIERY preacher, John the Baptist, who had baptized Jesus, had preached against the evils of the time. An opportunity came when Herod Antipas, King of Judea, took Herodias, his brother Philip's wicked wife. John the Baptist denounced the evil pair openly before the people, saying: "It is not lawful for Herod to have his brother's wife." Then the wilful Herod had the hermit cast into prison, but he feared to kill him, because the people revered him.

Now the day arrived when the birthday feast of Herod was to be celebrated, and he sat at a rich banquet in the midst of his Galilean nobles. Then came Salome, daughter of Herodias, lithe and beautiful. Fascinated by the dancing of his false wife's daughter, Herod roared: "Upon my oath, so greatly have you pleased me that I will give you whatsoever you ask, even if it be half of my kingdom!"

Then Herodias whispered into her daughter's ear, and the damsel came before the king and said: "Sire, give me on a platter the head of John the Baptist.

Herod regretted the rashness of his promise, but he could not retract it. So he issued his order to the prison. John was slain, and his head was brought to the dancer on a silver platter.

When the disciples heard of John's death, they came and took the prophet's body and laid it gently in a tomb.

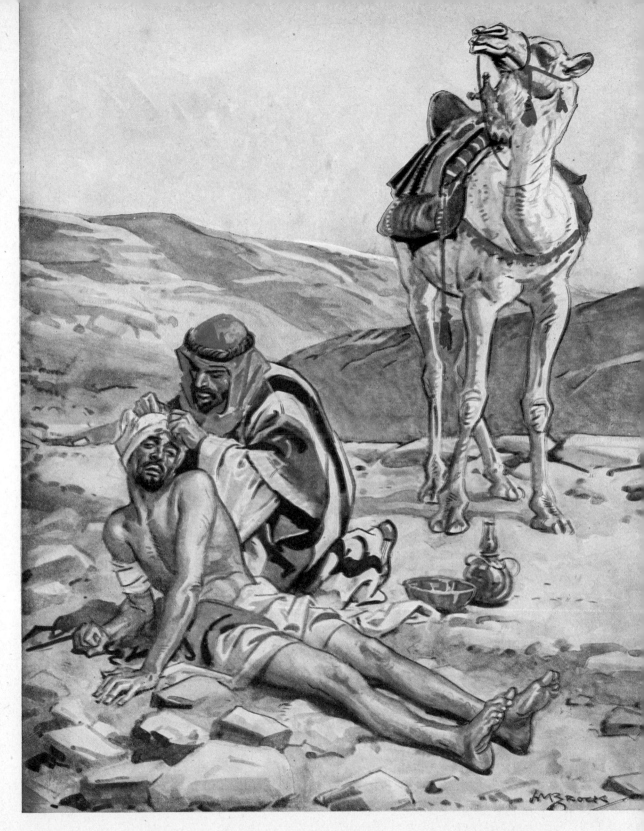

When he saw the wounded man, the Samaritan went over to him. (Page 163)

He sat down and spoke to the people from the ship. (Page 167)

The Five Loaves

WHEN JESUS LEARNED OF JOHN THE BAP-
tist's martyrdom, He took a boat across the lake to
a desert place to be alone. But the people discovered where
He had gone and followed Him on foot, bringing their
sick with them.

Jesus, seeing how many there were, was sorry for them.
He went out to them, spoke with them, and healed the
sick.

When it was evening His disciples said, "This is a desert
place and it is late. Send the crowds away so that they may
go to the villages and buy food."

Jesus answered, "They need not depart. You shall give
them to eat."

The disciples, wondering, answered, "But we have here
only two fishes and five loaves of bread. How can these
feed so many?"

Then Jesus said: "Have the people sit down in companies of fifty on the greensward."

Taking the five loaves and two fishes, Jesus blessed them
and broke them into pieces. He gave them to His disciples,
who, in turn, passed them out to the people. And they all
ate and were filled.

Later the fragments of the meal were gathered up, some
twelve basketfuls, although they who had eaten numbered
about five thousand.

The Storm on the Lake

THEN JESUS ORDERED HIS DISCIPLES TO take the boat and cross to the other side of the lake to Bethsaida while He sent the crowds away. When they were gone, He prayed there by Himself in the evening.

The ship was only about halfway across the lake when a sudden storm burst over the disciples as they toiled at the oars. They were making no progress, when they saw, walking over the waves, the figure of a man.

When the disciples saw him in the distance they cried out in fear, "It is a spirit."

But the figure, who was Jesus, said to them, "Be of good cheer; it is I. Be not afraid."

Peter called out, "Lord, if it is really You, bid me come to You on the water."

Jesus answered, "Come," and when Peter got down out of the ship and started to walk to Jesus, he saw how wild the waves were. He was terrified, and beginning to sink, he cried out, "Lord, save me!"

Immediately Jesus stretched forth His hand and caught him, saying, "O you of little faith! Why did you doubt?"

When they arrived at the boat, the wind ceased and the water became calm. And the disciples cried out to the master:

"Truly, you are the Son of God."

The Servant and the Debts

ONE DAY PETER CAME TO JESUS AND ASKED Him: "Master, if my brother sin against me, how often shall I forgive him? Till seven times?"

Jesus answered: "Not until seven times, but until seventy times seven." And He told this parable to illustrate how all men should hold in their hearts forgiveness for their fellow men:

"There was a certain king who, in going over his accounts, found that one of his servants owed him 10,000 talents. Since the man had no money with which to pay his debt, the king ordered him, with his wife and children, to be sold as slaves, so that payment might be made.

"The servant fell down before his lord and begged: 'Only have patience with me, and I will pay all.' So the king was moved with compassion, and he freed his servant and canceled his debt.

"Straightway this same servant went forth and found one of his fellows who owed him an hundred pence. Seizing him by the throat and shaking him, he cried: 'Pay me what you owe me!' And because the man could not, he had him cast into prison.

"Now, when others came to the king and told him what the servant had done, the king summoned him and said:

'O wicked servant, I forgave you even as you asked it of me. Should you not also forgive your brother?'

"Then, very angry, the king sent his servant into slavery until he should repay his debt."

A Rich Man's Heritage

ONCE WHILE JESUS WAS TEACHING A great company of people, a young man called out to him: "Master, speak to my brother, for he will not divide his inheritance with me!"

Then Jesus said: "I am not a judge over you. Beware of covetousness, for a man's life does not consist alone of the things which he possesses."

And Jesus spoke in a parable:

"The ground of a certain rich man brought forth abundantly, and he thought: 'Where can I store all my goods? I will pull down my barns and build greater ones. I will take my ease. I will eat, drink and be merry.'

"But God said to the rich man: 'You fool, this very night you shall die. Then whose shall these things be which you have hoarded?'

"So is he a fool who lays up treasure for himself, and is not rich in godliness. Therefore, take no thought for your life, what you shall eat, nor for your body, what you shall put on. Consider the ravens, for they neither sow nor reap, yet God feeds them. Consider the lilies of the field. They toil not, neither do they spin, yet Solomon in all his glory was not arrayed like one of these.

"But seek first the Kingdom of God, and all these things shall be given you."

With Publicans and Sinners

THE TAX-GATHERERS OF THE TIME OF Jesus were hated bitterly by all of the people. Therefore, the Pharisees murmured when Jesus and His disciples were wont to visit the dwelling of Matthew, the tax-gatherer, and to sit down at meat with the publicans and sinners who came to be taught. "Can He be such a good man, if He consorts with sinners?" the Pharisees asked one another.

But the Master knew their thoughts, and He said: "What man is there among you with an hundred sheep, who, if he lose one of them, would not leave the ninety and nine and go into the wilderness to seek the one which had strayed? And when he found it, would he not lay it upon his shoulder, and bring it home, and call to his neighbors to rejoice with him that the lost had been found?

"I say unto you, there is likewise more joy in heaven over one sinner that repents than over ninety and nine who have not sinned.

"Again, what woman, having ten pieces of silver, if she lose one piece, does not light a candle, and sweep the house, and seek diligently till she find it? And when she has found it, does she not call to her friends: 'Rejoice with me, for I have found the piece which I had lost'?

"Likewise, I say unto you, there is joy among the angels of heaven over every sinner that repents!"

The Prodigal Son

THE PHARISEES WERE ELDERS OF THE TEMple who believed that everyone should follow strictly the many laws and rules laid down for the people. They said of Jesus, "This man preaches that all should be good and follow the laws of the Lord. Then He talks and even eats with people who disobey the laws."

Jesus, hearing their complaint, told them the story of the Prodigal Son:

A certain man had two sons. The younger one said to his father, "Father, give me now the share of goods and money which will be mine some day." So the father divided the goods between the two brothers.

Not many days later, the younger brother gathered all his belongings together and went away. He traveled a long way and settled in a far-off country. He spent his money very foolishly and soon had wasted it all.

A great famine spread through that land, and soon he had nothing to eat. So he went to a citizen of the country to ask for work. The man sent him into the fields to herd his swine. The young man was so hungry that he could almost have eaten the corn husks that were given to the pigs. But no one gave him any food.

Thinking to himself, he said one day, "How many of my father's hired servants have not only enough to eat but plenty to spare? And here I am nearly dying of hunger.

"I will go home to my father and will say to him, 'Father, I have been very stupid and have done a great many foolish things. I am not worthy to be called your son. But let me be one of your hired servants.'" So he turned his face once more toward home.

When he was still a good distance from the house, his father saw him and ran to meet him, throwing his arms about the young man and kissing him.

But when the son asked to become a hired servant, his father instead called to the servants and said, "Bring out the best robe and put it on him. Put a ring on his hand and shoes on his feet. Then fetch a good fat calf and kill it. Prepare a feast. Let us eat and be merry, for my son has come home."

Now the elder son was working in the fields. When he

heard music and dancing, he came to see what was taking place. He called one of the servants to ask, and, when the servant told him, he was very angry and would not go into the house.

His father came out and asked the elder son to come to the feast.

But the son answered, "For all the years that he has been away, I have worked here at home with you. I have done nothing to worry you and have never disobeyed you. Yet you have never killed a fatted calf for me so that I might make merry with my friends. But as soon as your younger son returned, he who wasted everything you gave him, you prepared a feast."

And his father answered, "Son, you are always with me. Everything that I have is yours. I thought your brother was dead or lost. But he is alive and is found and is with us again, so it is right that we should be merry."

The Rich Young Man

IT CHANCED ONE DAY THAT A WEALTHY young man, richly clad, approached Jesus and asked: "Good Master, what shall I do to achieve eternal life?"

Jesus replied: "If you will enter into life eternal, keep the commandments."

"But all of these have I kept from my youth up," exclaimed the young man. "What still do I lack?"

Then Jesus, perceiving that he was very rich in worldly goods, said: "One thing you still lack. Go, sell all that you have and give it to the poor, and you will have treasure in heaven." Sorrowfully the young man went away, for many were his possessions.

Turning to His disciples, the Master said: "Verily, I say unto you, it is easier for a camel to go through the eye of a needle, than for a rich man to enter the kingdom of heaven."

Then Peter said: "Master, we have left all to follow after You." And Jesus answered: "There is no man who has left his home, his parents, brothers, wife or children for My sake, who shall not receive them again an hundredfold, for he shall inherit eternal life."

Suffer Little Children

ONE DAY IN THE TEMPLE, JESUS TOLD A story to certain of the congregation gathered there who felt that they were very righteous, and better in God's eyes than others.

"Two men went into the temple to pray, the one a Pharisee, and the other a publican.

"The Pharisee stood and prayed thus: 'God, I thank You that I am not like other men I see about me, unjust and dishonest, or like that publican. I fast twice a week, and make contributions to the temple.'

"The publican, standing near the back, did not even lift his eyes toward heaven but, bowing down, said, 'God, I pray that You will have mercy on me, for I know that I often do wrong things.'

"I tell you, this is the man who went home having found favor in the eyes of God. For those who praise themselves shall be abased, while those who are humble shall be exalted."

When he had finished speaking, the mothers brought their infants and little children and asked that Jesus touch them and bless them. The disciples, knowing that He was busy teaching, told them not to bother Jesus.

But Jesus called them to Him. He took the children up in His arms, put His hands on them and blessed them, saying, "Suffer little children to come to Me, and forbid them not, for of such is the Kingdom of God.

"You have often asked me, 'Who is the greatest in the kingdom of heaven?'

"Truly I tell you—unless you become as little children, you shall not enter the kingdom of heaven. The one who becomes as simple as a little child, he shall be exalted in the kingdom of heaven.

"Whoever is good to one such little child in My name, is also being good to Me. And whoever harms one of these little ones who believe in Me, would do better to hang a millstone round his neck and drown himself in the middle of the sea."

The Talents

ONE OF THE LAST PARABLES WHICH JESUS told his disciples was that of the talents:

"The kingdom of heaven," He said, "is like a certain man who was about to travel into a far country. He called his servants and gave to one five talents, to another two, and to the third one, according to the ability of each, and then departed on his journey.

"Now the servants who had received the five talents and the two talents traded with them and doubled their principal. But he who had received one talent dug a hole in the ground and hid it.

"After a long time the lord returned from his journey, and the three servants came before him for a reckoning. The first said: 'Master, you gave me five talents. Behold, I have earned you five more.'

And the lord said: 'Well done, good and faithful servant, you have been faithful over a few things; I will make you ruler over many. Share my happiness with me!'

"Likewise, he that had received the two talents came bearing four, and his lord was well pleased.

"Then came the third servant, and he said: 'Master, I remembered that you were a hard man, reaping where you have not sown, and gathering what you have not winnowed. So I was afraid you would charge me with careless stewardship. I hid your talent safely in the ground. Here, I return it to you as it was.'

"Angrily the lord cried: 'You wicked and slothful servant, you should have earned another talent with that one which you received. Give it to my servant who has ten talents, for to him who hath shall be given, and from him that hath not shall be taken away even that which he has.' "

And as Jesus talked the disciples were troubled in their hearts, for never had the Master spoken with such deep earnestness.

Palm Sunday

AS THE DISCIPLES TRAVELED TOWARD JERUsalem that last spring of the Master's life on earth, they were on the eve of great events. Unknown to them, in the city the enemies of Jesus were plotting the murder of the Lord.

Jesus and the disciples arrived at the outskirts of the vil-

They saw. walking over the waves, the figure of a man. (Page 170)

The young man was so hungry that he could almost have eaten the corn husks that were given to the pigs. (Page 175)

lage of Bethany, near the Mount of Olives, six days before the Feast of the Passover.

In the house of Simon, Mary anointed the Master's head and feet with ointment, and then He dispatched two of His disciples, saying: "As you enter the village you will see a colt which has never been ridden, tied near its mother. Loose it and bring it to me. If anyone asks you your purpose, say, 'The Master requires him.' "

So the disciples hurried toward Bethany, and at the fork in the road they found the colt, even as Jesus had said. When they had brought him to Jesus, they spread their robes upon the colt for a saddle, and the Master mounted him. Then they started down the Mount of Olives.

The people, who had heard Jesus preach and who had seen the miracles He had performed, gathered about Him. Some spread their clothes on the road before Jesus. Others cut down branches from the palm trees, waved them in the air, and strewed them in His path.

As Jesus and the disciples went their way, more and more people joined them, for many were journeying to celebrate the Passover Feast in Jerusalem. Those who knew Jesus told of all His mighty works that they had seen, and the people began to rejoice and to praise God with loud voices.

Thus they entered Jerusalem with rejoicing and proceeded to the temple.

When Jesus stepped through the portals of the temple, He saw the merchants busy with buying and selling, and the money changers bending eagerly over their tables, and He cried: "Is it not written that My house shall be called a house of prayer, and you have made it a den of thieves!"

Fashioning a scourge of small cords, He whipped the wrongdoers out of the temple.

When the high priests heard of this they plotted ways and means of putting Jesus to death, but seeing that the people loved Him, they dared not to touch Him. And thus in the evening Jesus returned unhindered to the peace and quiet of Bethany.

On the third day Jesus went again to the temple. The blind, the lame, and the sick from all Jerusalem came also, and He healed them. They went out from the temple healed, joined by the little children, crying out: "Hosannah to the Son of David!"

The chief priests and the elders came to listen while Jesus taught.

Once, thinking to trap Jesus, one of them asked Him, "By what authority do you say and do these things?"

Jesus said:

"I will answer you with a question. If you can answer Me, I will tell you by what authority I do these things.

"When John baptized, was it the baptism of heaven or of man?"

They reasoned among themselves: "If we say 'Of heaven,' then we will have all the people against us. For not all men believe that John the Baptist was a prophet."

So they answered, "We cannot tell."

Then Jesus said to them, "Then neither can I tell you by what authority I do these things."

Once more, thinking to trap Him into saying something that could be called disloyal to Caesar, they sent some of their followers to ask Him another question.

They asked, "Do you think it is right for us to pay tribute to Caesar?"

Jesus, realizing that they were trying to trap him, said, "Why do you tempt Me, you hypocrites? Show Me the tribute money."

They handed him a penny piece that bore Caesar's image on it. "Whose is this image and this name?"

They answered, "Caesar's."

Jesus said to them, "Render therefore unto Caesar the things which are Caesar's, and to God the things which are God's."

Silenced, they marveled at Jesus' answer and went away, for He had not fallen into their trap.

The Last Supper and the Betrayal of Jesus

JESUS PREACHED IN THE TEMPLE EVERY DAY, but at night He and His disciples went up to Mount Olivet to rest and pray.

It was nearing the time of the Passover feast, and while the chief priests and the scribes wished to kill Jesus, they dared not do it on such a great feast day, lest the people be angered and rise against them.

But Judas Iscariot, one of the twelve disciples, went to the chief priests and offered to bring them to where Jesus would be on the night of the Passover feast. There they would be able to arrest Him when He was alone with His disciples and the people would not be about. The chief priests were overjoyed and agreed to give Judas thirty pieces of silver for the betrayal of his friend.

The day of the feast came, and the disciples asked Jesus, "Where shall we prepare the Passover feast?"

Then Jesus sent Peter and John to prepare it. He said

to them, "Go into the city. There a man shall meet you, carrying a pitcher of water. Follow him into the house he enters and say to the master of the house, 'Where is the guest chamber where the Lord shall eat the Passover feast with His disciples?' He will show you a large room on the second floor. There make things ready."

Accordingly, the two set forth, and at evening the Master came with the rest, and they all sat down to begin the feast of the Passover.

As they were eating, they were suddenly startled to hear Jesus say, "One of you is about to betray Me."

Now Jesus had already warned His disciples that He would be arrested and killed and that the chief priests and rulers would persecute them because they had been His good friends and followers.

One by one, the disciples, in sorrow, cried out: "Is it I?" "Is it I?" For it seemed to each—except Judas—that none of them would turn against the Master.

Jesus answered, "It is one of you twelve."

Then He took some bread, blessed it and broke it. Giving it to His disciples, He said, "Take and eat. This is My body which is given for you. Do this in remembrance of Me."

Then he took the cup of wine, and when He had given thanks for it, He drank from it and then passed it around the table so that each one of them should drink from it.

And He said to them, "This is My blood which is shed for many. I will drink no more of this fruit of the vine until that day when I drink it with you in My Father's kingdom."

Then all of the disciples again inquired of Jesus which one would betray Him, and Peter said: "Lord, I shall not betray You! I am ready to go with You to prison or to death."

Jesus answered: "I tell you, Peter, this very night before the cock crows twice, you shall three times deny that you know Me."

Meanwhile, Judas had risen quickly to his feet and had slipped out into the night.

It was about midnight when Jesus and the eleven returned to Olivet and into the garden of Gethsemane. Then He said: "Tarry here and watch, while I pray yonder, for My heart is heavy with sadness."

Then He went off and threw Himself on the ground and prayed: "Father, if it be possible, let Me be spared this agony. Nevertheless, Your will, not Mine, be done!"

Returning, He found His disciples asleep, and He said, sadly: "What, could you not watch with Me even for an hour?"

Three times He came back to them, and each time He found them asleep, for they were worn out with sorrow and watching. When Jesus came to them the third time, He said, "Rise and let us go, for the one who is to betray Me is here."

And while He was yet speaking, a great crowd came swarming into the garden, bearing lanterns and torches and swords and staves. At their head was Judas Iscariot.

Then Judas said: "Hail, Master!" and kissed Him.

The kiss was the prearranged signal, and the soldiers immediately seized Jesus. As they did so Peter drew his sword and struck off the ear of one of the men. But Jesus rebuked the disciple: "They that take the sword shall perish by the sword. Do you not know that I could pray to My Father and He would send Me twelve legions of angels?"

And He touched the soldier's ear and healed it.

Then the soldiers dragged Jesus away, and His disciples fled into the darkness.

Jesus Before the High Priests

THE MOB DRAGGED JESUS TO THE HOUSE of Caiaphas, the high priest. There they sought to prove that their prisoner was a lawbreaker, but their witnesses, who lied, became confused and contradicted one another.

Finally one said: "This fellow, Jesus, has threatened to

tear down the temple and build another in three days without hands."

Then Caiaphas, the high priest, turned to Jesus and said: "Is this true?" But Jesus only held his peace.

Another testified: "He says that He is the Christ, the Son of God." And Jesus answered: "You have spoken the truth!" Then Caiaphas shouted: "He blasphemes. He deserves to be put to death!"

So they buffeted Him about and spat in His face.

Now Peter had followed on the edge of the crowd, and as he passed into the court, the damsel at the gate called out: "This man was with Him." But Peter, frightened, replied: "It was not I." And as he did so, the cock crew.

As Peter stood warming himself over some burning coals, a man looked earnestly at him, and cried: "Here is one of those disciples!" But again Peter denied the accusation.

When accused for the third time, Peter once more denied knowing the Master. And once more he heard the crowing of the cock.

Remembering how Jesus had foretold His beloved disciple's faithlessness, Peter wept bitterly and departed.

The Trial Before Pilate

IT WAS CERTAIN THAT THE SANHEDRIN OF Caiaphas would find Jesus guilty. But the sentence of death could be executed only with Roman approval, and Pilate, the Roman governor, would not listen to the false religious charges of Caiaphas. Only matters of treason against the state interested him.

So, when Jesus was taken to the judgment hall before Pilate, and the Roman demanded to know what accusations His captors wished to bring against their prisoner, they answered: "He is stirring up our whole nation against Herod's rule."

When Pilate's examination proved Jesus innocent, the governor suggested that He be flogged and released. It was the season of the year when, according to custom, one prisoner could be freed, and he said Jesus should be that one.

At this the crowd howled: "No, no! Crucify him! Set Barabbas free! But crucify this so-called King of the Jews!"

When Pilate saw that he could not prevail upon the mob, he took a basin of water and washed his hands before them all, saying: "I am innocent of the blood of this good man."

"Let His blood be upon our heads and upon our children's," the mob answered. And so Pilate, wishing to please the people, released Barabbas, a rioter and murderer, and turned Jesus over to them to be crucified.

Later that day, in a lonely place, a man tormented by remorse flung his thirty pieces of silver into the air and hanged himself.

It was Judas.

The Crucifixion

THE SOLDIERS OF THE GOVERNOR TOOK Jesus into the great common hall, pulled off His clothes, and put on Him a scarlet robe. They made a crown of braided thorns and placed it on His head, and put a reed in His right hand.

Then they bowed down before Him and mocked Him, saying, "Hail, King of the Jews!" And they spat on Him and struck Him.

When they had tired of the sport, they took off the scarlet robe, gave Him His own clothes, and led Him away to crucify Him.

As they went on the way, they took a man from the crowd, Simon of Cyrene, and forced him to help Jesus carry the heavy wooden cross.

There came the chief priests and scribes and their followers, also great crowds of people who had witnessed the good Jesus had done, and many women mourning for Him. But Jesus turned to them and said, "Daughters of Jerusalem, weep not for Me. Weep for yourselves and for your children."

At last the summit of Calvary, the Hill of the Skull, was reached. Here once more Jesus was stripped of His clothes. And here they nailed Him to a cross beneath the inscription, "The King of the Jews." And at the same time they crucified two common thieves, one on the right and one on the left. While the soldiers cast lots for His garments, a cup of vinegar was offered Him to drink.

"If you are the Son of God," jeered the mob, "come down from the cross."

But in His agony, He still prayed for His enemies: "Father, forgive them, for they know not what they do."

One of the thieves, as death drew near, repented, and Jesus reassured him: "Today you shall be with Me in Paradise."

At midday a sudden darkness fell over the city, and it lasted for three hours. In this gloom Jesus spoke four times. Once He said: "My God, my God, why have You forsaken Me?" Once in His agony, He cried: "I thirst!" Then He whispered: "It is finished." Finally, in a clear voice, Jesus prayed: "Father, into Thy hands I commend My spirit."

And at that moment an earthquake rent the veil of the temple, and the centurion who was standing guard, filled with awe, exclaimed: "Truly, this was the Son of God!"

When the soldiers came to determine whether those who had been crucified were no longer alive, one of them thrust a spear into the side of Jesus. Water and blood issued from the wound.

When evening came, Joseph of Arimathaea, a rich man who had been a follower of Jesus, went to Pilate and begged that he might have Jesus' body to bury it. Pilate commanded that the body be delivered to him.

Joseph bought fine linen, and in company with Nicodemus took down Jesus' body and wrapped it in the linen with fine spices, according to the custom of the Jews. In the garden near by they buried Him in a sepulcher hewn out of a huge stone, in which no one had ever been buried. Then they rolled a great stone against the door of the sepulcher.

The chief priests and the Pharisees went to Pilate, saying, "Sir, we remember that while Jesus lived He said, 'After three days I will rise again.'

"Command therefore that a guard be set over the sepulcher, lest His disciples come at night, steal His body, and say to the people, 'He is risen from the dead.'"

But Pilate answered, "You have your guards. Go your own way—make it as safe as you can."

So they went, sealed the stone at the door of the sepulcher, and set a guard by it.

Mothers brought their children, and asked Jesus to touch them and bless them.
(Page 178)

The blind, the lame, and the sick from all Jerusalem came, and He healed them.
(Page 182)

Easter Sunday

AS THE SUN WAS RISING ON THE FIRST DAY of the week, there came to the sepulcher Mary Magdalene, a woman whom Jesus had saved, and Mary, the mother of James, and other women who had come with Jesus from Galilee. They brought sweet spices with which to embalm the body of the Savior.

To their amazement, they saw that the great stone had been rolled away from the door of the tomb. Entering the sepulcher, they saw that the body of Jesus no longer was there. And sitting where the body had lain were two men dressed in shining garments, white as snow. And they were very frightened. But the strangers in white said: "Be not afraid. You seek Jesus of Nazareth Who was crucified. He is risen. He is not here. Behold the place where they laid Him. Go quickly. Tell His disciples that He is risen from the dead, that He has gone ahead to Galilee and that there they shall see Him, as He told you."

Running quickly, Mary Magdalene brought Peter and

John to the tomb, but there they found only the linen cloths with which Jesus had been bound. Then the disciples returned home, wondering, but Mary stood alone by the sepulcher, weeping.

Suddenly a voice behind her said: "Woman, why do you weep?" Turning, she saw someone standing there. It was Jesus, but she knew Him not, thinking He must be the gardener. "Sir," she replied, "if you have carried Him away, tell me where you have laid Him."

Jesus said: "Mary! Mary!" And falling at His feet, the woman cried out: "Master!"

Then He said: "Touch Me not, for I am not yet ascended to My father. But go to My brethren and tell them that I have arisen."

Again in the afternoon Jesus appeared to two of His disciples as they walked in the country. They went and told it to the rest, but still they did not believe.

Some people heard these things and told the chief priests, who then assembled with the elders and the scribes to take counsel. Then they called the soldiers whom they had put on guard and said, "Tell the people that the disciples came by night and stole away Jesus' body while you slept. We will pay you well, and if the governor should hear of it and send to punish you for sleeping on duty, we will speak to him and save you." So they did as they had been told.

That same evening, ten of the disciples were gathered together at supper in Galilee. The doors and windows were shut for fear of the people, and Jesus stood in their midst and said to them, "Peace be unto you." Then He showed them His wounds, so they knew it was He.

And He said to them, "Go to all the world and preach the gospel to every creature. Those that believe shall be saved, but those who do not believe shall be lost."

On another evening, when all eleven of the disciples were gathered at meat, they told Thomas that Jesus had visited them in the flesh. But Thomas was skeptical. "Except I shall see in His hands," he said, "the print of the nails, and thrust my hand into His side, I will not believe."

Then, again, the doors and windows being closed, Jesus came into the room where the disciples were and said: "Peace be unto you!"

And this time Thomas believed, crying out with joy: "My Lord and my God!"

Then Jesus said to the one who had doubted: "Thomas, because you have seen Me you believe: but blessed are those who have not seen, yet have believed."

The Last Breakfast

SEVERAL DAYS LATER, AT DAYBREAK, WHILE the disciples were fishing on the Sea of Tiberias, Jesus appeared to them on the shore. But the disciples knew Him not.

"Have you any meat?" He asked. They answered: "We have none."

Then He said: "Cast your net on the right side, and you shall catch something." And when they had done so, they could scarcely pull it in, it was so heavy with fishes. "It is the Lord!" cried John to Peter.

But some of them were fearful, thinking that they saw a ghost. Then Jesus said: "Be not troubled. Behold My hands and My feet with the nail wounds. A ghost does not have flesh and bones, as you see Me have."

With great joy they came ashore where there was a little fire laid, and fish broiling over the coals. And Jesus said: "Come and eat."

Then He asked Simon Peter: "Simon, do you love Me more than these?" Simon answered: "Yes, Lord." Then Jesus commanded: "Feed My sheep."

A second and a third time he asked this same question, and Simon was grieved.

"Master," he said, "You know all things. You know that I love You." Jesus said once more: "Feed My sheep!"

Then in the joyful light of the sunrise Jesus took His last leave of His disciples, promising them, "Lo, I am with you always, even unto the end of the world." And with a final blessing, He vanished forever from their sight.

A light shone in the prison, and an angel appeared before Peter. (Page 197)

As he fell to the earth, he heard a voice saying, "Saul, Saul, why do you persecute me?" (Page 199)

Peter's Escape From Prison

WHEN HEROD SAW HOW THE CHRISTIAN church was thriving under the teaching of the disciples and the apostles, he began to persecute them. First he put James to death with the sword. Then he had Peter arrested and cast into prison, where he was chained in an inner dungeon, guarded by soldiers.

Day and night, without ceasing, the church prayed for Peter. On the night before the day when Herod was to deliver him over to the mob, the disciple lay sleeping in the prison, chained between two soldiers.

Suddenly a light shone in the prison, and an angel appeared before Peter, saying: "Arise quickly!" And as he did so, the chains fell from his hands. Then the angel said: "Put on your garments and bind your sandals. Follow me."

As in a dream, Peter obeyed. So they passed the first and second guards and reached the iron outer gate of the prison, which opened of its own accord, and they passed through it into the city streets. Then the angel vanished.

Rejoicing that God had delivered him, Peter went to the house of Mark's mother, where many were gathered to pray for him. He knocked at the wicket in the gate. When the damsel Rhoda came and heard his voice, she ran joyfully to tell the others that Peter stood without. A few moments later all were rejoicing together.

The Voice From Heaven

FROM THAT TIME THE FOLLOWERS OF THE apostles rapidly multiplied, and their persecution at the hands of the people increased, also. Many of them, to avoid persecution, moved away and were scattered through Judea and Samaria. Some of the priests of the temple followed the teachings of Jesus, but the chief priests, the elders, the leaders of the Hebrews, did not. And, whenever they had the opportunity, they attacked the apostles.

One of the most faithful and fearless followers of Jesus was a young man named Stephen. He was stoned to death by the high priests and their followers.

Among those who had been foremost in the stoning of Stephen was a certain Jew of great education and prominence named Saul of Tarsus, afterward Paul. He went into every house where he thought there was a follower of Jesus and brought these men and women before the council, which sent them to prison.

One day when Saul was preparing to journey from Jerusalem to Damascus, he went to the high priest of the temple. Saul asked for letters to the chief priests of the synagogues in Damascus which would give him permission to bring back in chains to Jerusalem any men or women he might find there who were followers of Jesus.

As he approached Damascus, suddenly a great light from

heaven blazed about him. As he fell to the earth, he heard a voice saying, "Saul, Saul, why do you persecute Me?"

Trembling, he asked, "Who are you, Lord?"

The Lord answered, "I am Jesus whom you persecute."

Then Saul, astonished, asked, "Lord, what should I do?"

The Lord said to him, "Arise and go into the city, and it will be revealed to you what to do." And the men who journeyed with Saul stood speechless, hearing a voice but seeing no man.

Saul arose from the ground, and when he opened his eyes he saw nothing, for he had been struck blind. The others led him by the hand and brought him to Damascus.

For three days Saul could not see. Neither would he eat nor drink, but prayed to the Lord.

Then the Lord appeared in a vision to Ananias, one of His disciples in Damascus, and told him: "Go to the street called Straight, and inquire at the house of Judas for one Saul of Tarsus. I have chosen him to preach my gospel to many people."

Ananias answered, "Lord, I have heard how much evil this man has done to Your followers in Jerusalem. And here he has authority to carry back as prisoners all who call on Your name."

But the Lord said, "Go on your way. For I have chosen him to bring My name to the Gentiles, and kings, and the children of Israel."

So Ananias went his way to the house where Saul was staying. He put his hands on Saul and said, "Brother Saul, the Lord, even Jesus, Who appeared to you on your way here, has sent me to restore your sight and to bless you with the Holy Spirit."

Suddenly it seemed to Saul as though scales had fallen from his eyes, and he received his sight again. He arose and was baptized. Then he spent several days with the disciples who were at Damascus. Afterward he went to the synagogues and preached that Jesus was the Son of God.

All the people who heard him were amazed and said: "Is not this the man who destroyed those that called on the name of Jesus in Jerusalem?"

And with such fervor and earnestness did Saul preach in Damascus that the chief priests met in council and decided to kill him, and they set guards at the city gates lest he escape. But the other Christians took Saul by night and let him down over the city wall in a basket.

Saul returned to Jerusalem to join the disciples there. But they were all suspicious of him and could not believe that he was now one of them. It was Barnabas who took him before the apostles and told them how Saul had spoken with the Lord, and how boldly he had preached at Damascus in the name of Jesus.

Then they believed him, and he joined them and in humility changed his name to Paul, which means "little."

They placed a crown of thorns on His head, and made Him carry the cross.
(Page 190)

They saw that the great stone had been rolled away from the door of the tomb.
(Page 193)

The Persecution of Paul

PAUL AND BARNABAS PREACHED IN MANY lands and in many cities, and often they healed the sick.

In Lystra they healed a man who had been a cripple from birth. When the populace witnessed this miracle, they cried: "The gods have come down to us in the form of men!" And Barnabas they called Jupiter, and Paul, Mercurius.

But scarcely had the apostles won over the Greeks of Lystra to their teachings, when certain Hebrews came from Antioch and stirred up the citizens against the two Christians. Paul was driven out of the city and stoned and left for dead.

As his followers gathered about him, however, Paul arose to his feet and went along with them, preaching and healing.

Upon another occasion, in Thyatira, in Macedonia, Paul and Silas, another apostle, were followed about the streets by a demented slave girl, who brought great profit to her owners by her ability to tell fortunes. Pitying the maiden, the apostles healed her. When her masters saw that their hope of gain was gone, they seized Paul and Silas and dragged them before the city officials, charging them with false teaching. The magistrates ordered them stripped and flogged and placed in stocks in the inner prison.

At midnight, as Paul and Silas were praying, their prison suddenly was shaken by an earthquake which opened the doors and broke the prisoners' fetters. The keeper awoke from sleep to see the doors standing open, and supposing all his prisoners had escaped, he drew his sword to slay himself. But Paul cried: "Stay! Do yourself no harm. We are all here."

Then the keeper lighted a torch, and in fear and trembling, threw himself at the feet of the apostles. "What must I do to be saved?" he cried.

Paul and Silas then preached the word of God to the jailer and all his family, and baptized them.

In the morning the magistrates, having learned that their prisoners were Roman citizens, hastened to have them released, and soon afterward Paul and Silas left the city of Thyatira.

Journey's End

MANY WERE THE ADVENTURES OF PAUL during his stay in the Mediterranean lands. Everywhere he was hounded by those who sought to have him brought to trial and executed as a heretic. At length they succeeded in having him taken prisoner and placed on a ship bound for Rome, where he and other prisoners were to be brought before Caesar for judgment.

When the ship was barely out of sight of land, a storm arose, and the wind blew with such terrific force that the captain could not steer his vessel and almost ran ashore on an island. As the storm continued unabated, the crew threw overboard the cargo, and finally even the ship's gear. The sun and the stars were hidden for days, and the food dwindled until there was none left for the hungry voyagers.

When the sailors had given up all hope, Paul, who had spent the time in fasting and prayer, came on deck and said: "Be of good cheer. God has appeared to me in a vision and promised that, though we lose the ship, we are safe."

At daybreak they sighted an inlet, toward which they steered. But as they came near shore, a swift current caught the vessel and ran it aground, where it was at the mercy of the pounding waves. The captain commanded all who could swim to strike out for shore, and by seizing planks and other wreckage, the entire company were washed to the beach. And all were saved, even as Paul had promised.

The shore upon which Paul and his shipmates had been cast belonged to the island of Melita. The day was rainy and cold, and the castaways built a great fire on the beach. As Paul was casting faggots on the fire, a viper, driven out by the heat, fastened its poisonous fangs in his hand.

Then the natives cried: "This man must surely be a

murderer, for, though he has been saved from the sea, vengeance yet will slay him."

But Paul merely shook off the viper into the flames. He had not been harmed. Since he did not fall dead, the natives decided that he must be a god.

The governor of the island, Publius, received the castaways very hospitably in his home, and there Paul found Publius' aged father lying sick of a fever. Paul, laying his hands on the sufferer, healed him, and later healed many others among the islanders who were sick.

When the time came for the strangers to leave, the grateful natives fitted out a ship for them, providing for all their needs.

After sailing for several months, Paul came to Rome, where he remained for two years, urging all who would hear him, both Jew and Gentile, to follow the teachings of Jesus Christ of Nazareth.

Thus the word of Christ was spread from the Eastern world to Europe, and the people who followed Christ's teachings became known as Christians.

The † End

GREECE

Athens

Smyrna

Rhodes

Crete

Cy

Alexandria

GOSHEN

Mt. S

Memphis

EGYPT

Nile River

Red Se

Bible Lands